Writing as a Thinking Process

Writing as a Thinking Process

Mary S. Lawrence
Under the Auspices of
the English Language Institute
at the University of Michigan

Ann Arbor

The University of Michigan Press

ISBN 0-472-08550-6
Library of Congress Catalog Card No. 78-185153
Published in the United States of America by
The University of Michigan Press and simultaneously
in Rexdale, Canada, by John Wiley & Sons Canada, Limited
Manufactured in the United States of America

1989   1988   1987   1986   13   12   11   10

Preface

Writing as a Thinking Process is the result of several years of experimentation in teaching composition to intermediate and advanced level foreign students at the English Language Institute, The University of Michigan. The book is based on an approach to writing which is semantic and cognitive. The method and the materials have been developed with the encouragement and support of the administration of the English Language Institute.

The book has four parts. The first, which is introductory and preparatory, introduces the method the student is to use. The following three sections progress from controlled writing to free writing. The exercises are cumulative in the sense that they use data and cognitive methods which have been presented in preceding lessons.

The data presented in the exercises are drawn from many sources, including a number of U.S. government publications. I gratefully acknowledge the permission to reproduce material granted by:

1. American Association for the Advancement of Science, publishers of *Science*.
2. National Tuberculosis and Respiratory Disease Association.
3. *The New York Times* Company.
4. Population Reference Bureau, Inc.

I wish to thank the students and teachers of the English Language Institute who tested the materials for their valuable suggestions. I would like to give special thanks to Professor Ronald Wardhaugh, Director of the English Language Institute, who read the final manuscript.

Contents

Contents

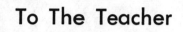

To The Teacher

Introduction

The text is designed for students of English as a second language of intermediate and advanced levels of proficiency. It is intended for persons who wish to learn English for academic, professional, or business reasons. It has been tested successfully with students ranging in age from 17 to 47 and of more than 30 different academic or professional backgrounds.

The text provides about 150 class hours of instruction (i.e., a two-semester course.) Not all students, however, will need to do every part of every exercise. Although it is assumed that the students will write in class every class session, some writing exercises can be assigned for homework. The text can thus be adapted to course time which is less than two semesters.

The exercises are designed to help the students develop an ever-growing competence in *expository* writing. There is no attempt to teach creative writing: description, fiction, or poetry. The method of teaching focuses on active intellectualization. The students are to be aware of the cognitive methods they are utilizing and be able to identify them. Moreover, they must make associations and relationships clear to the reader. The kind of written prose aimed at is that which is primarily *clear* and suitable for essay type examinations and reports. At the end of the course each student should be able to make clear to the reader his own individual patterns of thought. The emphasis on synthesis lays the foundation for research writing.

General Principles

The text is based on an approach to writing which is semantic and cognitive. Providing for active transfer of each student's knowledge of grammar and vocabulary, it bridges the gap between controlled writing and free writing. Semantic in emphasis, this system of teaching composition focuses on writing as a means of communication. The writing practice is concerned with meaning, both in content and through relationships. The cognitive method treats writing not as an end-product to be evaluated and graded but as an activity, a process, which the student can learn *how* to accomplish. Pedagogically, it relies on active thinking, that is to say, on a conscious awareness of the intellectual process. It capitalizes on the students' ability to think inductively and on the cognitive skills they already have. In everyday life, they impose order on data by a variety of cognitive methods, such as categorization, equivalence, contrast, and causality. They have also had experience in formulating different kinds of generalizations and extrapolations. The exercises lead the students to identify the methods of thinking they have at their disposal and to apply them to writing. A detailed account of the general theoretical principles of cognition on which the text is based can be found in the writings of Jerome S. Bruner of the Center for Cognitive Studies, Harvard University. Briefly, this approach to writing is an enquiry method, in which the students ask questions, manipulate data, and extrapolate from data.

3

Students are provided with data and, as a consequence, with the vocabulary they need in order to write. From the outset they are asked to formulate questions based on the data. The practice in question framing is intended to produce the habit of formulating logical questions which can be used in attacking any expository writing assignment.

Similarly, from the outset, the students must formulate statements of inference. Drawing inferences and extrapolating from data allow for a wide variety of student responses. The formulation of inferences does more than provide for individual student differences, however; it is an essential part of the enquiry method on which the materials are based. As the students work with the data, they are able to make more and more complex associations and extrapolations.

In addition to framing questions and inferences, the students manipulate data and engage in problem-solving. At the simplest level, they impose a specified kind of logical order on data. They practice writing according to a sequence of logical methods of ordering data, and progress to written problem-solving which entails active recall of data, and more and more sophisticated syntheses of data.

This system of writing attempts to maximize each student's intellectual participation in the writing process. It requires memorization and active recall. More importantly, it demands that each student be at all times engaged in an internal dialogue. He must be actively aware of the goals he is attempting to achieve and of the cognitive methods he is utilizing. Thus, writing as a process of active thinking is inextricably linked to student independence and student accountability.

The Subject Matter Areas

Throughout the text the students are provided with data to manipulate and to write about. The information they are given deals with subject matter areas which were chosen because they are topics in which educated persons are interested. They are basic topics, such as government, history, transportation, communications, nutrition, economics, and general science. Material which is likely to be new is included to provide motivation.

The information was selected to provide useful vocabulary: words, phrases, and sentence patterns which will be of use to the students after the course is completed, because of their wide general applicability.

Cycling of Subject Matter Areas

Data about the various general topics, such as communications, transportation, government, and so on, are not organized in units or in chapters. The information is presented in recurring cycles to ensure a maximum of vocabulary retention. The cycling of subject matter areas forces the students to recall both vocabulary and ideas. The instructions repeat the necessity for active recall throughout the text.

The teacher may not wish to read the detailed instructions aloud for each and every exercise. However, he must urge the students to actively recall vocabulary and ideas from earlier exercises. It may sometimes be necessary to point out which earlier exercises are relevant. The practice of active recall should become a habit.

The cycling of subject matter areas also allows for synthesis and more sophisticated extrapolation: the students can draw on a variety of former exercises for ideas and examples; they can choose from these and augment their choices from their own personal store of data. Since the ability to combine data and ideas from a variety of sources logically and fluently is an absolute necessity for the expository writer, one of the major aims of the text is to develop a facility for synthesis.

Vocabulary

Vocabulary acquisition, vocabulary retention, and vocabulary utilization are crucial for any writer, and are particularly important for the person writing in a language other than his native tongue. This text provides the students with the vocabulary they need in order to write. The sequence of exercises is organized to force the students to review and use again vocabulary they learned in earlier assignments.

It is assumed that the students will learn vocabulary items because they use them and then later must recall these items and use them again. Therefore, the teacher should *not* assign vocabulary lists for memorization. Instead, the students should be encouraged to develop the habit of consulting previous lists and exercises.

The vocabulary throughout is divided into two kinds: *content* vocabulary (dealing with subject areas) and *structure* vocabulary (dealing with relationships). The students must understand the distinction.

The vocabulary includes, as far as possible, several ways of expressing the same ideas; it is particularly important for students to learn a variety of ways to express each logical relationship. The teacher must urge each student to utilize a variety of expressions in his writing and to *choose* to practice the least familiar or most difficult. It is each student's responsibility to learn vocabulary, to practice it, and to make choices.

The Logical Methods of Written Organization

The exercises provide practice in identifying a sequence of logical relationships and in using these relationships to impose order in writing.

The students formulate questions which focus on the logical relationships; the questions they write must correspond to the type of answer designated. The students manipulate data; they impose order on the data according to designated logical methods of organization. Each relationship is practiced first in isolation in short compositions. Later assignments demand a synthesis of logical methods of imposing order on the data. Finally, each student chooses and combines methods of organization independently.

Writing practice moves from (1) sentence and question writing, to (2) compositions in which the method of organization is practiced in isolation, to (3) compositions which demand a combination of methods of organization. The ultimate aim is writing in which each student *actively chooses* the ways in which he imposes order on the information he is dealing with.

The logical methods of organization — classification, definition, and so on — are, by and large, those found in most rhetoric texts. However, the approach to teaching these methods of organization differs from that of conventional rhetoric books. In this text there are no model paragraphs and no model compositions. The students arrive at the concepts inductively. The text avoids the artificiality of the composition assignment which is wholly classification or wholly comparison and contrast — a type of writing which many rhetoric books demand. The emphasis is on enquiry, on synthesis, and on choice. The text seeks to utilize the cognitive skills the students have at their disposal and to make them aware of them in writing.

The methods of organization are arranged in order of increasing difficulty for the non-native speaker of English. Hypothesis, for example, is introduced late in the course because of the difficulties students encounter with the *if* construction.

Many of the logical relationships overlap, of course. Classification is a form of contrast; prediction is a kind of cause-and-effect inference; chronological order and causality are related. The teacher can point out these inter-relationships to the students. It is not necessary, however, to become involved in an elaborate, esoteric discussion of logic. In fact, such discussions are to be avoided as they detract from the writing practice. The students must, however, master the meta-language of the course; that is to say, they must be able to identify and name the logical methods they are practicing.

Provision for Student Differences

The text allows for individuality in student response and for different levels of student ability. The teacher must be willing to accept a variety of answers. Since the text progresses from teacher-directed writing to student-directed writing, it also allows for ever-increasing individualization.

1. The emphasis from the outset on writing inferences based on the data permits a variety of student response. The teacher should take time for discussion of the inferences the students write; some will be simple, others will be ingenious and sophisticated, but the only criterion of correctness is logical possibility. Each student should be able to explain his reasoning. The teacher must be open to understanding his reasoning, and must adopt a positive encouraging attitude towards student answers.

6

2. The exercises in manipulation of data can usually be answered in more than one way. For example, when the students are asked to classify data, there are many possible methods, some obvious, some not so obvious. The teacher will be happily surprised at some of the interesting responses the students make.

3. Many of the exercises demand a facility in joining sentences. Here, again, a wide variety of correct responses is possible. Students should be encouraged to utilize a variety of methods of sentence transformation and embedding. Students who favor *and* and *but,* for example, can be told to keep a count of their use of these connectors and to reduce the number. The exercises allow for individual choice in sentence sophistication; all students, however, should be encouraged to aim for a degree of variety in their sentence-style.

Talking about Writing

If the students are to derive maximum benefit from this approach to writing, the proportion of class time spent talking about writing must be minimal. As the course goes on, less and less time should be devoted to class discussion. The students must understand what they are doing at all times. Pre-writing discussion is, therefore, mandatory, but need not be lengthy, particularly after the course is well under way. Similarly, a limited amount of class time should be planned for group discussion of student responses, for example, of the inferences the students extrapolate from the data. Since the exercises allow for a wide variety in student answers, all the students may benefit from occasional sharing of individual responses. But regardless of how interesting class discussion may be, the bulk of class time should be devoted to writing.

Pronunciation

The teacher must allow time for pronunciation practice of key words and phrases introduced in the exercises. This need not take up a large percentage of classroom time. Rapid oral repetition of new words should become a class habit. If the students are to recognize new vocabulary and to retain it, they must know what it sounds like.

Throughout the text the students read silently while the teacher reads aloud. In this way they are exposed to the data through two senses. Moreover, this method ensures constant attentiveness.

Presenting New Vocabulary

After reading the material aloud to the students, and practicing the pronunciation of relevant words, the teacher should allow a few minutes for discussion of new vocabulary. The students should be helped to figure out meanings from context; occasionally additional explanations may be required.

The class time devoted to vocabulary discussion should be held to a minimum. The materials are designed to help the students acquire and retain vocabulary by active recall and utilization. Lengthy discussion of vocabulary will ensure neither vocabulary acquisition nor fluent writing.

Grammar

The text assumes that intermediate or advanced-level students have a degree of proficiency in English grammar. Unlike many composition books, this text is not grammar-based; the focus is on communication and meaning, not on grammatical analysis. But a semantic approach cannot exclude all references to grammar. Each of the logical relationships the students practice has its own series of associated grammatical patterns. To write fluently using chronological order, for example, the students require a mastery of tenses; hypothesis demands a facility with the peculiarities of *if* clauses, and so on. The teacher may wish to review particular grammatical points relevant to the exercise at hand before the students write.

Similarly, the vocabulary of certain subject matter areas may raise grammatical problems for the non-native speaker — for example, pronoun substitution, count and non-count nouns, and preposition choice. Here again, the teacher should point out relevant grammatical difficulties, and should encourage student questions during in-class writing. The students soon learn to ask for information about the accurate use of nouns like *news* and *means* in the exercises concerned with communications; about preposition choice after such words as *consist* and *related;* about possessive forms in statements of contrast and comparison; and about the difference between *good* and *goods* and *rise* and *raise* in the business and economics exercises. Moreover, the classroom teacher should help the students arrive at answers to some of their grammar questions by examining the sentences in the text.

The Paragraph

The text teaches paragraphing inductively. There are no model paragraphs, no arbitrary rules of paragraph division, and no artificial rules about "topic" sentences. The exercises are designed to help the students arrive at the concept of the paragraph independently. They are asked to group data into associated units and practice each logical method in isolation; these activities help form the habit of dividing written ideas into separate units.

The teacher should stress paragraph separation. This convention can be taught in the opening exercises where the necessity for paragraph division is less and where, if more than one paragraph is called for, the division is easily identified. The teacher should indicate the need for paragraphing when necessary in correcting papers.

Since the concept of "the paragraph" is not one for which we can devise an indisputable formula, the teacher can best convey the idea of paragraph unity by making suggestions about what the students have already written rather than by talking about a hypothetical model of perfection.

8

The text avoids the term "topic" sentence, favored by so many approaches to composition teaching. Instead students are given sentence patterns suitable for paragraph openings. In addition, they have at their disposal summary sentences in the different kinds of generalizations (generalizations of classification, contrast, causality, etc.). Through these generalizations and the inferences they extrapolate from the data, they can arrive inductively at the concept of a topic sentence or summary sentence. This concept is extremely helpful to the student writer of exposition. But since a topic sentence is not an indispensable ingredient of every good paragraph, students should not be told that every paragraph they write must have one, or that all good paragraphs have topic sentences, or any such generalization. Each student's paragraphing should be a reflection of his own logical patterns of thought.

Writing Speed

From the outset, students must be encouraged to work quickly. Depending on the class level of ability, a time limit can be set for the completion of some assignments. It is essential to establish a pattern of student awareness of the necessity for working quickly. Students should keep track of how many words they write in a specific block of time. They should aim for around 250-300 words in thirty minutes.

In-class Writing and Homework

It is assumed that the students will write in class every day. Regular practice is essential. While the students are writing in class, the teacher should circulate making corrections and suggestions. Students should be encouraged to ask questions about spelling, idiom, vocabulary, etc. during the classroom writing period. Every effort must be made to avoid an "examination-atmosphere": the object of the writing exercises is not to test the students but to help them learn *how* to write.

The teacher may wish to assign some of the writing exercises for homework. Exercises which have not been introduced and discussed first in class should never be assigned for homework. The students should be given some indication of how many words their homework assignment should include and how much time they should spend on a homework assignment; it is a good idea to indicate a maximum cut-off time. To foster student accountability the students can be asked to record for each homework assignment the time spent and the approximate number of words.

Assignments

1. The teacher must not omit the exercises which introduce each of the logical methods of organization.

2. The teacher must not omit the structure vocabulary for any of the logical

9

methods of organization. Similarly, every student needs practice with the suggested sentence patterns.

3. The teacher must be aware that the later exercises demand *recall* and *synthesis.* If one student omitted an early exercise about a certain topic, say pollution or nutrition, he should complete it before writing a composition which demands recall and synthesis of data on that topic. The students need the CONTENT vocabulary and the IDEAS from the earlier exercises on any given topic.

4. Students who are extremely proficient may not need to do every part of every writing exercise. For example, the text provides a great deal of practice in sentence writing. Some students may not need so much practice. Similarly, there are many exercises dealing with each logical relationship. The teacher may wish to give some assignments on an individual basis.

5. The text deals with a variety of subjects. Here, too, the teacher may wish to make individual assignments, giving the students appropriate topics according to their academic interests. Not every student, for instance, benefits from the exercises related to biology. Each student should know the generally useful vocabulary, however, from *all* the exercises.

6. In the later exercises, particularly the discussion exercises, the students should be allowed to choose which compositions they wish to write.

Correcting the Student Papers: Teaching not Testing

Ideally, the students will write in class daily, and their corrected papers will be returned to them the next day. They should be held responsible for correcting their errors. It seems pointless, however, to ask students to copy and recopy their papers. Copying requires little active thought. A more fruitful method is to ask each student to write new correct sentences, eliminating errors, whether they be grammatical constructions, idiomatic phrases, or vocabulary choices. This method serves the double purpose of allowing the teacher to determine whether or not the particular student understands the correction and of facilitating active transfer.

The text emphasizes teaching not testing. The teacher should focus on improvement and development. In other words, the teacher's attitude should be positive; student writing should not be measured against a hypothetical standard of perfection. Most importantly, the teacher must realize that correcting papers, evaluating student writing, and assigning grades is not the primary aim of the writing class: teaching students *how* to write is!

Explanatory
and
Preparatory
Exercises

Explanatory Exercises

Exercise One

> Read silently while your teacher reads aloud. "Repeat in
> your mind" what your teacher reads.

The composition exercises in this book are based on the assumption that writing is
a form of communication and that the process of writing is an active thinking
process. These exercises demand a high degree of intellectual involvement on your
part. You are asked to think before you write and while you write.

In the exercises a distinction is made between CONTENT (that is to say, subject
matter) and LOGICAL ORGANIZATION (that is to say, method of organization).
You are asked to concentrate on two things: *what* you are saying and *how* you
are organizing what you are saying.

The exercises are about a wide variety of topics. The subject matter areas were
chosen because they are interesting and also because they provide the kind of vocabulary an educated English-speaking person knows. Students of English as a second
language who use this book will probably go on to study at an English-speaking
university or use English in business or professional life. The content areas provide
the kind of vocabulary you need to know.

The exercises are about a wide variety of topics. At first you may think the subject
matter content is random, but this is not so. The subject matter content is arranged
to allow for vocabulary review. Therefore, all the exercises about air pollution are
not placed together, one after the other. All the exercises about government are not
placed together, one after the other. If the exercises using one kind of content
vocabulary were all in one section, you might forget the vocabulary when you
finished the section and started a new one on another different topic.

The exercises distinguish between CONTENT and ORGANIZATION. Throughout
the book you will learn a number of basic logical methods of organization that are
common in English writing. When you are thoroughly familiar with the different
logical methods of organization and the vocabulary you need to express your ideas,
then you will be able to apply these methods of organization in your writing to any
subject. Furthermore, you will be able to choose and to combine different methods to
achieve fluency and logic. The end result will be your own individual expression.

A. Divide the following into two groups — one group of subject matter, the other group of methods of logical organization. (You may use your dictionary if you wish.)

air pollution   prediction
cause and effect   economics
American history   hypothesis
chronological order   biology
government   classification
comparison   nutrition

B. The following are some of the kinds of logical organization you will practice in this book.

Match each one with its definition.

chronological order
prediction
comparison
classification
contrast

Telling in advance what will happen; to foretell.
Stating similarities.
Stating differences.
Arranging events in order according to time of occurrence.
Systematically grouping into categories that have similar characteristics.

Exercise Two

> Read silently while your teacher reads aloud. "Repeat in your mind" what your teacher reads.

As you do the exercises in this book, you will learn a lot of vocabulary. You will expand the active vocabulary that you need in order to write fluently. Some of the vocabulary you know already; some will be entirely new to you. You will learn different ways of expressing the same ideas so that you can achieve more variety in your writing.

This is not a sleepy way to learn vocabulary. You must be alert all the time. The method you will use has been designed to help you increase your memory span so you can retain a larger vocabulary. You will be asked to *actively recall* the vocabulary presented in the exercises. It is up to you to *choose* to use the vocabulary.

In the exercises, vocabulary is divided into two kinds: (1) content vocabulary and (2) structure vocabulary. Content vocabulary is made up of the words and phrases you need to write about a particular subject. For example, if you are writing about

14

government, there are certain words you need to use. Structure vocabulary is the vocabulary you need when you write about relationships. Whenever you write consecutive prose, you use a method of organization as well as content. Structure vocabulary includes words and phrases for comparison and contrast, words and phrases for chronological order, and so on.

Before you write you will be asked to *actively recall* the content vocabulary. You will also be asked to *actively recall* structure vocabulary. When you write, you will *choose* the vocabulary you want to use. If you force yourself to try to remember vocabulary, you will increase your memory for English. If you are an ambitious student eager to learn English, you will *choose* to practice new ways of expressing yourself. As you progress through the exercises, you will learn more and more different ways of expressing yourself in English.

A. Read the following sentences. Indicate which are TRUE and which are FALSE.

1. The method of learning vocabulary used in this book is so easy that the students don't need to work.
2. One fundamental principle of the exercises is active recall.
3. All the vocabulary in this book will be new to the average student.
4. Recall is a synonym for remember.
5. Students don't need to remember structure vocabulary.
6. Content vocabulary refers to the subject matter of the exercises.
7. Students have no choice in the vocabulary they can use in the exercises.
8. If a student uses the active recall method, his memory span will decrease daily.
9. Structure vocabulary is the vocabulary of architecture.
10. There is only one correct way to express an idea in English.

B. 1. In this book you will learn content vocabulary. Examine the following groups of words. Give a general content topic for each group. (There may be more than one appropriate answer.)

CONTENT VOCABULARY	TOPIC
Example:	
children, school, curriculum	education

1. news, T.V., newspapers, reporter
2. energy, work, vitamins, meals
3. color, sculpture, painting, appreciate, museum
4. vote, election, president
5. train, airplane, passport, ticket
6. factory, manufacture, profit
7. money, bank, deposit, interest
8. rain, crops, cultivate, food

2. Write one sentence for each group of words.

Example: The school provides a suitable curriculum for the children.

C. The exercises in this book have two kinds of vocabulary: content vocabulary and structure vocabulary. Match the vocabulary in column A with the type of vocabulary in Column B.

COLUMN A	*COLUMN B*
the amount of protein	Structure: comparison
presidential veto	Content: weather
in my opinion	Structure: substantiation
prior to the war	Content: government
wind velocity	Structure: personal opinion
for example	Content: nutrition
similar to	Structure: cause and effect
censorship of newspapers	Content: fine arts
sculpture	Structure: chronological order
as a result	Content: news media

This matching exercise shows that content vocabulary can be applied to more than one subject. For example, *wind velocity* is vocabulary used in talking about *weather,* but it is not restricted to meteorology. Airline pilots, sailors, and many other people use the phrase. Much of the content vocabulary you will learn is useful in more than one subject area. All of the structure vocabulary is useful in every subject area.

Exercise Three

> Read silently while your teacher reads aloud. "Repeat in your mind" what your teacher reads.

The composition exercises in this book are based on the assumption that *writing is a form of communication* and that *the process of writing is an active thinking process.* Because you will become familiar with the content of the exercises, your ability to *paraphrase* (to reword) will be increased.

Because you will practice using logical relationships, you will be able to apply these relationships and methods of organization in all kinds of writing.

From these exercises, then, you will get subject matter ideas and vocabulary and also methods of organization. But nobody wants to spend all his time writing paraphrases of other people's ideas. The exercises will teach you to make *associations* and *inferences,* and to look for implications. In your compositions you will combine:

> CONTENT from the exercises
> LOGICAL ORGANIZATION from the exercises
> YOUR OWN ASSOCIATIONS and INFERENCES

The exercises do not ask you to copy unthinkingly. You will be asked to recombine and rework the content. You will be given data and asked to manipulate the information. At all times you must be awake and actively aware of what you are doing. You will *consciously choose* vocabulary, ideas, relationships, and logical organization. The end result will be your own individual expression.

A. Write sentences about the material you have just read. You will be given:

1. the topic
2. an indication of whether your sentence is to be TRUE or FALSE

TOPIC	*SENTENCE*	*TRUE/FALSE*
paraphrase	Example: Learning to paraphrase is stupid.	False
inferences		True
choosing vocabulary		False
data		False
copying without thinking		True

B. When we make an inference from data, we come to a conclusion. We decide about additional information by ourselves. We think about the data that we are given; then we INFER that something else is true.

For example:

If I know that Mr. Smith has ten children and that Mr. Smith has a very small car, I can infer that

Mr. Smith is poor.

or

Mr. Smith's car will be very crowded.

or

Mr. Smith has another bigger car too.

or

The Smith family does not need to use a car very often.

Not everything I infer is necessarily TRUE; sometimes my inference may be ERRONEOUS. Sometimes our inferences are FACTS; sometimes they are OPINIONS. Obviously, the more data we have, the more accurate our inferences can be.

17

Write an inference for each of the following.

1. There is smoke coming from the house next door. The fire-engine is outside.
2. Mr. Smith is carrying a suit case. He is entering the bus station.
3. Mrs. Jones is holding a gun in her right hand. Mr. Jones is lying on the floor. Mr. Jones is dead.
4. It is late at night. Mr. Johnson's dog is barking.
5. My alarm clock is ringing.

Exercise Four

> Read silently while your teacher reads aloud. "Repeat in your mind" what your teacher reads.

The exercises in this book are composition exercises. They are designed to help you write more fluently. You may be surprised, then, to find that your teacher will ask you to practice the *pronunciation* of words and phrases in each exercise. If you are to master the vocabulary so that you feel comfortable using it, it helps to know what the words and phrases *sound like*. Pronunciation practice will also help you recognize the vocabulary when you hear it.

Similarly, you may be surprised that your teacher will read the exercise aloud to you while you read silently. This method is used to help you *actively concentrate* on the material in the exercises. It will expand your memory span, extend your listening recognition of English, and help you to figure out meaning from context. While your teacher is reading aloud, you are reading, listening, and thinking, not just resting!

These are the instructions you are to follow.

> A. Read silently while your teacher reads aloud. "Repeat in your mind" what your teacher reads.
>
> B. Try to understand meanings from context. Think first. Then ask your teacher for meanings you don't understand.
>
> C. Repeat the pronunciation of words and phrases your teacher will pronounce aloud.

The instructions are enclosed in a box. They will appear in many of the exercises to help you remember the system you are to follow.

Repeat the following words and phrases after your teacher. Each word or phrase refers to a METHOD of writing you will practice.

chronological order	comparison	prediction
spatial order	contrast	hypothesis
inference	analogy	personal opinion
generalization and substantiation	cause and effect	persuasion
anecdote	explanation	refutation
classification	definition	discussion

Exercise Five

> Read silently while your teacher reads aloud. "Repeat in your mind" what your teacher reads.

Understanding information in a foreign language is not easy. Writing about that information in a foreign language is not easy either. You cannot absorb information the way a sponge absorbs water. To understand and to write in English you must carry on a continuous "thinking" process. You must take facts and opinions and arrange them, relate them to each other, and organize them. You must draw inferences from them. One key to developing these skills is to ask questions and to answer questions. In order to facilitate your understanding of data you should actively ask questions.

The number of individual questions you can ask is infinite, but the kinds of questions are not. In this book you will find many exercises in which you are asked to write questions rather than answers. These exercises are to help you practice a method of understanding information in English — a method that should become a habit.

A. Indicate the response (or responses) which do not answer the following questions. Be prepared to discuss your answers.

Question: How . . .?   slowly
                                 with difficulty
                                 Mary
                                 fast
                                 in a hurry

19

Why . . .?	in order to
	because
	because of
	for _____
	in 1945
When . . .?	for one hundred miles
	six days ago
	a long way
	just around the corner
Where . . .?	in Chicago
	at the airport
	next to
	on State Street
	at home
Whose . . .?	Mary's
	that belongs to _____
	mine
	to me
Who . . .?	man
	mine
	six
	farmer
	Chinese
How many . . .?	sixty
	her
	dozen
	approximately _____
	hundreds
How long . . .?	for _____
	approximately _____
	for sixty _____
	not here
	for a short time
Which . . .?	the _____ one
	the red _____
	a house
	the other _____
	the big _____
What . . .?	ate it
	apples those
	something because
	ran the _____
	chair she

B. Match the following question words and phrases with the kind of answers you expect.

Who?	Actions, processes
Where?	Letters
What is he doing?	Numbers, weights,
What did he do?	measures
How? What is the way to?	Name of person(s)
How do you spell?	Method
How many? How much?	Locations
Why?	Time
When?	Reason

C. Match the following questions with the topics they are about.

1. Is it helpful to ask questions?
2. How should I learn vocabulary?
3. What constitutes a good diet?
4. Why should I manipulate data?
5. What curriculum does the school have for its students?
6. How many ways to communicate news are there in the U.S.?
7. Do you like sculpture or painting best?
8. Who can vote in the election?

government	fine arts
manipulation of information	learning vocabulary
news media	education
nutrition	asking questions

D. Match the following questions with the kind of answer you expect.

1. What should I do to learn to write fluently?
2. What is the difference between learning vocabulary and sleeping?
3. Why should I learn the pronunciation of new vocabulary?
4. How many kinds of structure words are there in English?
5. Is it interesting to write about a variety of topics?
6. Who can absorb water like a sponge?

yes/no	reason
number, classification	action, method
name of person(s)	contrast

E. Write questions about the following topics. Your question must fit the kind of answer designated.

TOPIC	KIND OF ANSWER
asking questions	yes/no
data	yes/no
asking questions	reason
learning information	method
good exercises	place, name of book
understanding English	action

Exercise Six

> Read silently while your teacher reads aloud. "Repeat in your mind" what your teacher reads.

Many students think that the most important aspect of writing is grammar. The exercises in this book focus on *what* you are writing about (content) and *how* you are organizing your writing (method). The exercises are not designed to teach grammar. All of the students who use this book have already studied English grammar. Most of you still make some grammar mistakes. The teacher will correct your grammar mistakes and your mistakes in spelling by giving you the correct forms. It is your responsibility to correct your grammar mistakes and to work on your own individual problems. The more you write and correct your papers, the better your command of written grammar will be. Practice writing new sentences using the forms correctly. Be *actively aware* of your own grammar problems when you write.

Some exercises involve certain grammatical forms. For example, in stating a hypothesis you must know how to write sentences using *if*. The teacher will point out those particular forms to you.

A. Match the following methods of organization with the grammar you should know for each method. Some items may fit more than one category.

prediction	future tense
hypothesis	past tense
spatial order	clauses of result
chronological order	prepositions in expressions
cause and effect	of direction
comparison and contrast	count and non-count nouns
classification	clauses using *if*
	adjective and adverb forms

22

B. In writing we distinguish between content and method. Even in single sentences we can distinguish between vocabulary which is content vocabulary and vocabulary which deals with logical relationships.

Indicate the vocabulary of logical relationships in each of the following. Then choose from the list below which kind of relationship each is.

1. Because smallpox is a communicable disease, people should be vaccinated.
2. Prior to becoming President, George Washington was a military man and a gentleman farmer.
3. There are three main branches of the U.S. federal government.
4. I would go to Europe if I had enough money.
5. The careers of John F. Kennedy and Abraham Lincoln have one aspect in common.

classification   hypothesis   chronological order
comparison   cause and effect

Preparatory Exercises

Active Recall

> Read silently while your teacher reads aloud. "Repeat in your mind" what your teacher reads.

The game of football is played between two teams of eleven men on each side. Any player can be replaced by a substitute from his team at any time in the game. Before the game begins, the referee tosses a coin up in the air in the presence of the captains of the two opposing teams. One of the team captains says, "Heads!" or "Tails!" The winner of the toss has two choices: either to choose which goal he wants to defend or to choose between kicking the ball first or receiving the kick-off. If, for example, he chooses to kick, then the other captain can choose the goal. The game begins when one team kicks the ball towards the opposite goal; this is called the kick-off.

After you have discussed any vocabulary you could not understand, try to RECALL the content of the passage. Do not look at the passage unless you absolutely have to.

Answer the following questions:

1. Who throws a coin in the air?
2. When does the game begin?
3. Who has two choices?
4. How many teams can play at one time?
5. What is a kick-off?
6. How many men are there on each team?
7. Does the referee say, "Heads"?
8. Are the captains there when the referee tosses the coin?
9. When can a player be substituted?
10. What are the two choices the one captain has?
11. When can the captain who does *not* win the toss choose the goal he wants?
12. In which direction does the team kick the kick-off ball?

Pronoun Reference

> Read silently while your teacher reads aloud.

The composition exercises in this book ask you to combine and rework data. You will be asked to manipulate information. To do this it will often be necessary to combine sentences.

When we combine sentences it is usually necessary to substitute *he, she,* or *they* for the names of people, and to substitute *it* or *they* for things. If we do not make these substitutions, our writing is very repetitious.

Complete the following three exercises. Draw arrows to show what the pronouns that are circled refer to.

A. On February 12, 1809, the son of Thomas and Nancy Lincoln was born. They named him Abraham after his grandfather. When he was fifteen years old Abraham was so tall and strong that he often worked on his neighbors' farms to earn money. Usually he took along a borrowed book to read while he ate his lunch. He kept it inside his shirt ready to read. He could work hard, but many of the neighbors said he was lazy. "Abe's always reading and thinking," they said. Abraham once answered, "My father taught me to work but he didn't teach me to love it."

B. Mr. Smith's desk is always very untidy. He can never find anything he wants in it. His wife says he's the most untidy, disorganized person she has ever met. His secretary agrees with her. They both smile whenever he shouts, "Where did you put my glasses?"

C. Many stories are told about the Greek philosopher, Diogenes. One day Alexander the Great came to visit him and asked him if there was any favor he could do for him. Diogenes replied that Alexander should not stand between him and the sun. Diogenes got rid of all his possessions except a purse and a wooden bowl. But he threw the latter away when he saw a boy drinking water from his hand one day. At another time he walked at noon in the streets carrying a lantern. When the people asked him why he was carrying it, he said, "I am looking for an honest man."

D. Write pairs of sentences using:

both   the former   the latter   each

Combining Sentences

A. About Nutrition

> Read silently while your teacher reads aloud.

The composition exercises in this book ask you to manipulate data. To do this it is often necessary to combine sentences. Usually, there are many possible correct combinations.

For each of the following write one sentence.

Example:

(a)   Living things need energy.
(b)   Energy comes directly from the sun.
(c)   Energy comes indirectly from the sun.

Sentence:

The energy needed by all living things comes directly or indirectly from the sun.

1. (a)   People get energy from the food they eat.
   (b)   The body stores food in a form that can be used later.
   (c)   Excess food is stored as fat.

2. (a)   Food helps children grow.
   (b)   Food gives people energy for work and play.
   (c)   Plants need food.
   (d)   Animals must have food.

3. (a)   Food produces energy.
   (b)   We measure energy in calories.
   (c)   A calorie is the amount of heat needed to raise one gram of water one degree Celsius.

4. (a)   Some people eat too many calories.
   (b)   Some people eat more food than they need.
   (c)   The body makes excess food into fat.

5. (a)   Some people do not eat enough.
   (b)   The body uses fat for energy.
   (c)   Some people lose weight.

6. (a)   Protein is necessary for good health.
   (b)   Protein is found in milk, cheese, meat, and eggs.
   (c)   Proteins are chemical compounds.

7. (a)   Carbohydrates supply fuel for the body.
   (b)   Fats supply fuel for the body.
   (c)   Fats and carbohydrates are made up of carbon, hydrogen, and oxygen.
   (d)   Fats are found in butter, oil, cream, and peanut butter.
   (e)   Carbohydrates are starches like cereals and potatoes.

8. (a)   Vitamins are necessary for health.
   (b)   There are many different vitamins.
   (c)   Lack of vitamins can cause disease.
   (d)   Many foods, like fruits and vegetables, contain vitamins.

B. About Government

Read silently while your teacher reads aloud.

The composition exercises in this book ask you to manipulate data. To do this it is often necessary to combine sentences.

There are many ways to combine sentences in English. Here are some ways you may want to use:

(a)   *and, but, or*
(b)   *which, of which,* etc.
(c)   *who, whom, whose, to whom,* etc.
(d)   words like *because, although, when,* etc.
(e)   changing word order

For each of the following write one sentence:

1. (a)   The Department of State is one part of the Executive branch of the U.S. government.
   (b)   The Department of Agriculture is one part of the Executive branch of the U.S. government.

(c) The Executive branch has many departments.

2. (a) U.S. citizens can petition to repeal laws.
   (b) U.S. citizens can petition to enact laws.

3. (a) The President approves or vetoes bills.
   (b) The President appoints Cabinet members.
   (c) The President appoints Supreme Court Justices.
   (d) The President makes treaties with foreign countries.

4. (a) The President has the power to propose foreign treaties.
   (b) Foreign treaties must be approved by the Senate.

5. (a) Bills to raise money through taxes must be introduced in the House of Representatives.
   (b) The Senate can amend tax bills proposed in the House.

6. (a) Members of the House of Representatives are chosen by vote every two years.
   (b) Senators are elected for six year terms.
   (c) The Congress has two parts.

7. (a) There are nine Supreme Court Justices.
   (b) Supreme Court Justices are appointed for life.
   (c) The President appoints Supreme Court Justices.
   (d) The appointment of a Supreme Court Justice must be approved by the Senate.

8. (a) Two senators are elected from each state.
   (b) Senators are elected for six year terms.
   (c) The members of the Senate work in Committees.

9. (a) Members of the House serve for two year terms.
   (b) Each state elects representatives according to its population.

10. (a) The U.S. government has three branches.
    (b) The Judicial branch interprets the law.
    (c) The laws are made by the Legislative branch.
    (d) The Executive branch enforces the law.

Make three other sentences combining any of the data you wish. For example, you may wish to combine 4 (b) and 7 (d).

C. About Air Pollution

Read silently while your teacher reads aloud.

The composition exercises in this book ask you to combine and rework data. You will be asked to manipulate information. To do this it will often be necessary to combine sentences.

There are many ways to combine sentences in English. Here are some ways you may want to use:

(a) *and, but, or*
(b) *which, of which, to which,* etc.
(c) *who, whom, whose, to whom,* etc.
(d) words like *because, although, when, where,* etc.
(e) changing word order

Examine the following data.

1.   Smoke is often dirty.
2.   Smoke is often gray or black.
3.   Smoke results from burning fuel.
4.   There is water vapor in smoke.
5.   Water vapor is invisible.
6.   There is carbon dioxide in smoke.
7.   Carbon dioxide is invisible.
8.   Solid particles of carbon are found in smoke.
9.   Solid particles of carbon are not invisible.
10. Solid particles of carbon and ash are called soot.
11. Smoke from wood is almost colorless.
12. Smoke from coal is black and oily.
13. Factories produce smoke.
14. Industrial smoke is usually dirty.
15. Industrial smoke pollutes the air.
16. In some cities the average amount of soot that falls is 80 tons per square mile every month.
17. Smoke dirties laundry, houses, streets, and even plants.
18. Sometimes smoke contains sulphur.
19. Sulphur in smoke corrodes iron and steel.
20. Sulphur in smoke kills plants.
21. Smog is smoke combined with fog.
22. Many people are worried about pollution from smoke.
23. Many people want to control the amount of smoke from industries.
24. Many people want industries to burn smokeless fuel.

Rewrite the material combining sentences. There are several ways you can do this; choose the method you consider the most logical. You may have one paragraph, or more than one paragraph. Try to use all the data you are given.

Making Inferences

Read silently while your teacher reads aloud.

The composition exercises in this book ask you to manipulate data. They also expect you to make INFERENCES in order to come to conclusions about the data you are given. You are expected to be alert to the IMPLICATIONS of the content material you are given.

When the passage gives you definite information we say the information is EXPLICIT. When the passage does not give you definite information, but you can figure it out from what you are given, the information is IMPLICIT.

A. Listen to the following passage.

> "Wanted – young, skinny fellows not over 18. Must be expert riders. Willing to risk death daily. Orphans preferred. Wages $25 a week."

This advertisement appeared in a Missouri newspaper in 1860. The boys who got the jobs became Pony Express riders. They carried the mail from St. Joseph, Missouri, to Sacramento, California. It was often a dangerous trip because of the weather and Indians. The fastest trip took 7 days and 17 hours for 2,000 miles. The average speed for mail delivery between Missouri and California was 10 days. The charge per half ounce was $5.00; consequently, most people wrote letters on very thin paper. The Pony Express was discontinued in October, 1861.

1. Answer the following FACTUAL questions:

   (a) Why did letterwriters in the 1860's use thin paper when they wrote letters to California?
   (b) Who became Pony Express riders?
   (c) How long did the Pony Express last?
   (d) How much shorter than the average delivery time was the fastest Pony Express trip?

2. Look at the questions and answers you wrote for question 1. For which of the questions did the passage give EXPLICIT information; for which was the information IMPLIED?

3. Write three statements of INFERENCE about the Pony Express based on this selection.

4. Read each of the following statements. Decide if it is TRUE or FALSE. Explain if you cannot decide because you have INSUFFICIENT EVIDENCE. Be prepared to give reasons for your answers.

(a) The Pony Express was a failure.

(b) The Pony Express delivered mail about two thousand miles.

(c) Most of the Pony Express riders were over eighteen years of age.

(d) All Pony Express riders were orphans.

(e) The Pony Express operated only in good weather.

(f) The Pony Express was replaced by the telegram.

(g) Before 1860 there was no regular mail delivery overland to California.

(h) The Pony Express riders rode at approximately five miles per hour.

(i) The Pony Express riders averaged two hundred miles per day.

(j) No women became Pony Express riders.

5. Why is it hard to decide if some of the statements are TRUE or FALSE?

6. Look at the answers you wrote for question 4. For which of the TRUE and FALSE statements did the passage give EXPLICIT information; for which was the information IMPLIED?

7. Examine the statements in the text for question 4 again. This time decide where each fits on this relative scale.

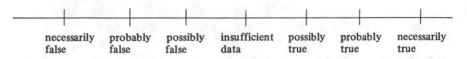

| necessarily false | probably false | possibly false | insufficient data | possibly true | probably true | necessarily true |

B. Examine the following inferences. Decide which are logical and which seem to you to be only possible.

ACTION	*INFERENCE*
1. Abraham Lincoln had very little education in school.	Lincoln was a stupid president.
2. Churchill lost the election in 1945.	Churchill was not popular.
3. Abraham Lincoln walked three miles to return six cents to a customer he had overcharged.	Lincoln was honest.
4. Thomas Edison was not a good student in school.	Edison was lazy.
5. From 1474 to 1492 Columbus tried to get money for his first voyage to the Indies.	Columbus was stubborn.
6. Queen Elizabeth I of England wore a different new dress almost every day.	Queen Elizabeth was proud and rich.
7. Sir Francis Chichester sailed around the world in a small sailboat.	Chichester was brave.

8. St. Francis gave all his money to the poor.　　　　St. Francis was foolish.

9. When Edison was a boy he made "a telephone" from bottles and wire.　　　　Edison was resourceful.

10. George Washington fought the British with a small army of poorly trained soldiers.　　　　Washington was foolhardy.

Which of the INFERENCES are FAVORABLE? Which are DEROGATORY? The inference says: Columbus was *stubborn.* Make the inference *FAVORABLE* by using a word like *persistent.* Do the same for the other DEROGATORY inferences.

C. Listen to the following passage.

Many times flu and cold germs are spread from one member of the family to another by the contamination left on dishes after washing. A dishwasher helps to relieve this problem by using scalding hot water, much hotter than could be used in hand dishwashing. So, not only do you have the convenience of automatic dishwashing but you will also be helping to protect your family's health.

1. Answer the following questions:

   (a)　Who is the paragraph meant to be read by?
   (b)　What is the purpose of the paragraph?
   (c)　Who do you think wrote the paragraph?
   (d)　What does the author imply about heat and germs?

The answers to the four questions are not EXPLICITLY stated in the paragraph. This information is IMPLICIT.

2. Write an INFERENCE about each of the following:

   (a)　cold germs
   (b)　dishwashers
   (c)　advertisements for dishwashers
   (d)　scalding water

3. Match the following adjectives and temperatures on the chart and then arrange them in proper order. Here is a clue:

   freezing = 32°F. or 0°C.

very hot	180°F.
freezing	60°F.
cold	212°F.
cool	140°F.
boiling	100°F.
hot	32°F.
warm	40°F.

Word:

$$\vdash\!\!\!-\!\!\!-\!\!\!-\!\!\!-\!\!\!-\!\!\!-\!\!\!-\!\!\!-\!\!\!-\!\!\!-\!\!\!-\!\!\!-\!\!\!-\!\!\!-\!\!\!-\!\!\!-\!\!\!-\!\!\!-\!\!\!\dashv$$

Temperature: 212°F.   32°F.
100°C.   0°C.

4. Some of the temperature vocabulary words you were given in 3 indicate RELA-TIVE values. Which words are RELATIVE? Which would you consider scientifically accurate?

D. 1. Write two sentences of INFERENCE about each of the following.

Mozart could play several musical instruments when he was five years old. Two years later he toured Europe giving concerts on the harpsichord and violin.

Achilles, a Greek hero, argued with his Greek leader about a girl. When he could not have the girl, he refused to help his friends in the war, even though his leader pleaded with him to fight.

Which of these two persons would you describe as *precocious?* Write a sentence using this word about another historical person. Some people say Achilles was *stubborn.* Is that a good thing to say about him or a bad thing? Words which tell us that the speaker approves have FAVORABLE connotations; words which tell us that the speaker does not approve have DEROGATORY connotations.

2. Choose a historical character. Write some facts about him. Read aloud what you have written to the class. The class will make an inference about the person's character. Decide if the inference is FAVORABLE or DEROGATORY. Here are some words you may wish to use for your inference:

foolish	depressed	an optimist
brave	optimistic	a pessimist
foolhardy	pessimistic	easy going
inventive	proud	creative
mechanical	vain	immoral
precocious	greedy	unscrupulous
strong	persistent	shrewd
cautious	obstinate	skillful

versatile	stubborn	technically skillful
curious	persevering	competent
scientific	musical	mean
flexible	talented	impartial
opportunistic	a hero	disinterested
sad	a prodigy	uninterested
homesick	a good writer	neutral
confused	a mechanical genius	(un)prejudiced

E. Listen to the following:

1. When Edison was six years old he wanted to find out how a bird came out of an egg. He found a nest of eggs and sat carefully on them. He spread his clothes over the eggs. He planned to sit on the eggs until they hatched. Soon his mother made him leave the eggs and his first experiment ended.

   Write two statements of INFERENCE about Edison when he was a child. (Try to remember content vocabulary from earlier exercises.)

2. Henry Ford was frequently bad in school. One day his teacher told him to stay after school. For a punishment he told Henry to put together all the pieces of a watch. Henry enjoyed the punishment. It took him ten minutes to reassemble the watch.

   Write two statements of INFERENCE about Ford as a boy. (Try to remember content vocabulary from earlier exercises.) Write two statements of INFERENCE about Ford's teacher.

3. Look at the INFERENCES you made about Ford's teacher. Decide where you would place them on this relative scale.

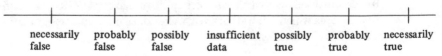

| necessarily false | probably false | possibly false | insufficient data | possibly true | probably true | necessarily true |

F. Make a LOGICAL INFERENCE about the following:

1. There are approximately 200,000,000 people in the U.S. Nearly 3 billion pounds of soap are produced yearly in the U.S.
2. Sound travels through air at 1,129 feet per second.
   Sound travels through water at 4,794 feet per second.
   Sound travels through iron at 16,820 feet per second.
3. In 1966 more than 25 million people attended 2,768 football games played by U.S. college teams. The football stadiums at several universities hold more than 75,000 spectators.
4. Softball is played with a ball which is twelve inches in circumference. The ball weighs about six ounces. The pitcher must throw the ball to the bat-

ter underhand. About ten million people play softball for recreation in the U.S. The game has different rules for the distance between bases for men and women (60 feet), and for girls and boys (45 feet).

Content vocabulary you may want to use:

produce	metal	professional
production	gas	amateur
consume	liquid	participate
consumer	solid	participant
consumption	velocity	popular
per capita	speed	popularity
	recreation	

From these exercises we can see that it is possible to make many, many inferences from a single piece of information. We must distinguish, however, between IN-FERENCES which make sense and those which do not.

When we write, we usually want the reader to know when we are INFERRING. The following sentence patterns can be used for inferences.

From _____ I can infer that _____ .
From _____ it seems to me that _____ .
I can safely guess that _____ .
On the basis of _____ we can say that _____ .
My inference is that _____ .
It seems likely that _____ .
         probable
         possible
From _____ I conclude that _____ .
From _____ I can assume that _____ .
It is safe to assume that _____ .
The evidence implies _____ .
The facts indicate _____ .
We can deduce _____ .
We can logically deduce _____ .
We can make a logical inference about _____ .
We can make a logical inference that _____ .

Writing Questions

> Read silently while your teacher reads aloud.

A. In 1620, after a 65-day voyage across the Atlantic, the Pilgrims landed on the coast of Massachusetts. The *Mayflower* carried 101 passengers and a crew of 43. The passengers, now known as Pilgrims, had sailed from England in the *Mayflower* in order to acquire religious freedom. The English King, James I, did not allow freedom of religion. Everybody was expected to belong to the state church, the Church of England. At first the Pilgrims had escaped to Holland in 1608. When they decided to start a colony in North America, they spent three years making preparations. They obtained a grant of land from the Virginia Company in London. Because they were poor, they could not afford to buy supplies for their new colony. They agreed to send lumber and furs back to the English merchants for seven years in exchange for supplies. The first ship they tried to sail on was not the *Mayflower*. They started off for America twice on another ship, but each time had to go back because the ship leaked. When they finally sailed, it was September 16, 1620, and the weather was very bad. The Pilgrims were the first colonists to write a document providing for a democratic government in the New World.

After you have discussed any vocabulary you could not understand, try to RECALL the content of the passage. Do not look at the passage unless you absolutely have to. Write questions about the content using the following patterns:

1. How long _____ ?
2. Who _____ ?
3. Why _____ ?
4. How far _____ ?
5. How _____ ?

6. How many _____ ?
7. When _____ ?
8. Where _____ ?
9. What _____ ?
10. How often _____ ?

B. Write questions about the following topics. All of the topics have been introduced in previous exercises. Try to recall vocabulary.

TOPIC

1. football
2. dishwashers
3. the Pilgrims
4. carbon
5. soap production
6. lumber

TOPIC

7. mail delivery
8. cold germs
9. foreign treaties
10. protein
11. fuel
12. Lincoln

Fact and Opinion

When we read, some of the statements we read are FACTS and some are the author's OPINIONS. Facts can be checked and proved. Opinions reflect the writer's own individual way of looking at life, including his way of looking at the information he is writing about. Opinions involve value judgments.

Similarly, when we read we make inferences. Some of our inferences are FACTUAL but some are OPINION.

For example, after I read about the Pilgrims I may decide:

(a) that the Pilgrims expected to find furs in America.
(b) that the Pilgrims were stupid to sail when the weather was bad.
(c) that the Pilgrims were brave.
(d) that the Virginia Company owned land.

Which of these are fact?
Which are opinion?

When we write, we should indicate when we are writing our opinions.

The following sentence patterns can be used to express opinions.

I think	seem (seemed) to be
It seems to me that	appear (appeared) to be
In my opinion	seemingly
To me	In my view
I consider	From my point of view
I claim that	According to me

A. Write a statement of FACT and a statement of OPINION about each of the following topics. All of the topics have been introduced in previous exercises. Try to recall vocabulary.

TOPIC	*TOPIC*	*TOPIC*
1. fat people	3. dishwashers	5. inventors
2. smoke	4. recreation	

Level One Exercises

Instructions

Read silently while your teacher reads aloud.

The exercises in this book increase in difficulty. Obviously the first exercises are easier than the later ones. In all the exercises you will be asked to manipulate data. At first you are provided with all the data. Soon you start making inferences and associations. In the later exercises you are expected to RECALL information and logical methods from the earlier exercises. In the final section of the book you have an opportunity to express personal opinion and to draw on your own personal "store of data."

In the beginning exercises you are asked to follow a system of

thinking *before* you write;
thinking *while* you write.

These are the instructions you are to follow for the beginning exercises.

A. Read silently while your teacher reads aloud. "Repeat in your mind" what your teacher reads.

B. Try to understand meanings from context. Think first. Then ask your teacher for meanings you don't understand.

C. Repeat the pronunciation of words and phrases your teacher will pronounce aloud.

BEFORE YOU WRITE:

A. RECALL IN ENGLISH what the exercise is about.
    REPEAT IN YOUR MIND the CONTENT information.
    REPEAT IN YOUR MIND the CONTENT vocabulary.

B. RECALL IN ENGLISH the method of written organization of the exercise.
    REPEAT IN YOUR MIND the STRUCTURE vocabulary.

> WHILE YOU ARE WRITING:
>
> A. DO NOT RELY ON COPYING. RETAIN in your mind what you are writing about and how it is to be written. Refer to the text only to refresh your memory.
>
> B. ASK YOURSELF QUESTIONS about the CONTENT and about the METHOD.

The instructions are enclosed in boxes. These instructions will appear in many of the exercises to help you remember the system you are to follow.

Introducing Chronological Order

Read silently while your teacher reads aloud.

Throughout this textbook you will learn a number of basic logical methods of organization. One of the most obvious methods of organization is to arrange information according to TIME SEQUENCE. In this text this kind of logical order is called CHRONOLOGICAL ORDER.

Arrange the following information about immunization in CHRONOLOGICAL ORDER.

1. In 1885 Pasteur developed a rabies vaccine that could be used for humans.
2. In 1941 a successful vaccine against typhus was developed.
3. The first vaccine, that against smallpox, was discovered in England by Jenner in 1796.
4. In 1955 a huge crowd gathered at the University of Michigan to hear scientists announce that a vaccine against polio had been developed and successfully tested.
5. Prior to the smallpox vaccine as many as 80,000 people died each year in England from smallpox.
6. In the 1950's there were about 30 diseases for which veterinarians had vaccines to use to prevent animal diseases.
7. Because no vaccines are perfect, work is still continuing to refine the vaccines we already have as well as to develop new methods of immunization.

Structure Vocabulary

The following is a list of *some* of the structure vocabulary you need when you write about chronological relationships.

    now, nowadays
    when
    before, after, while, during
    between _____ and _____
    in (year)
    since _____
    later, earlier, formerly, etc.
    every (number) (years, months, days, etc.)
    at the turn of the century (decade), etc.

in the first half of the century, etc.
in the 1900's, etc.
at birth, in childhood, in infancy, in adolescence, as an adult, in
       adulthood, in old age, at death
simultaneously, simultaneous with, at the same time as
former, latter
previous, previously, prior to
first, second, etc.
in the first place, in the second place, etc., to begin with
next, then, subsequently, in the next place
at last, in conclusion, finally

Composition Exercises

1. Chronological Order: Possible Order/Logical Order

In working with chronological order we arrange events according to time sequence. Sometimes there may be more than one possible method of arrangement. Then we should ask: Which is the most likely? Which is the most logical?

Possible Order and Logical Order

Combine the pairs of sentences in this exercise using *after, while,* and *before.*

Notice that you will probably want to use *he, they,* etc., in one part of your sentence. You may have to change verb tenses.

1. Mr. Jones flew to Chicago. Mr. Jones bought a ticket.
2. The student felt sick. The student ate ten hot dogs.
3. The dog bit the mailman. The dog ran out of the house.
4. The nurse ate her lunch. The nurse went to work at 2 p.m.
5. The man fell asleep in the auditorium. The lecturer spoke about avoiding boring topics.
6. Mary broke her leg. Mary went skiing.

In some cases, there may be more than one *possible* order. For example, the nurse could possibly eat her lunch after 2 p.m. Choose the order you think is most logical in each case.

2. Sentences Expressing Chronological Order

Write STATEMENTS of CHRONOLOGICAL ORDER to fit the following patterns. (You may use more than one word for the blanks.)

1. Prior to _____ I liked to _____ .
2. Before the turn of the century many people _____ .
3. In the 1900's people traveled by_____ ; later they _____ and now they can _____ .
4. To begin with you must _____ in order to learn to play the piano; next you must _____ .
5. In adolescence many boys _____ , but subsequently they _____ .
6. At the same time as_____ , _____ .
7. Before I learned about _____ , I thought that _____ .
8. Formerly I liked _____ , but nowadays I _____ .
9. During childhood I _____ , but now as an adult _____ .
10. Between 1900 and 1970_____ .

11. While I _____ , I used to _____ every day, but finally I _____ .
12. Since I was ten years old, I have _____ .

3. Chronological Order (U.S. History)

> Read silently while your teacher reads aloud. "Repeat in your mind" what your teacher reads.
>
> Try to understand meanings from *context*. Think first. Then ask your teacher for meanings you do not understand.
>
> Repeat the pronunciation of words and phrases your teacher will pronounce aloud.
>
> (To the teacher: Pronounce for the class words you choose from the exercises, words in the suggested vocabulary list, and words in the appropriate structure vocabulary list.)

In the United States today coffee is a more popular drink than tea, but tea played an interesting part in the early history of the U.S.A. Before the U.S. won its independence from Britain, the colonists had to pay a tax on tea which was brought into the country by ship. The colonists disliked paying taxes to Britain as the money was used to support officials who had been sent to America. In 1770 the British Prime Minister Lord North had repealed most of the taxes but George III had insisted on retaining the tax on tea. The king saw the tea tax as symbolic of the British right to tax the colonies. About nine-tenths of the tea imported into the American colonies after 1770 was not taxed because the colonists illegally smuggled it into the country. In 1773, however, the British parliament passed a new law which gave a British company the right to import tea cheaply to the American colonies. The American merchants were alarmed. They feared that the government might grant other monopolies. In Boston a group of citizens disguised themselves as Indians; they boarded the British company's ship and threw $15,000 worth of tea into the harbor. This active resistance against Britain is known as the Boston Tea Party.

A. Make a chronological chart of the events. Be sure you get all the important facts in the correct order.

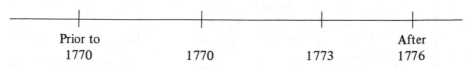

| Prior to 1770 | 1770 | 1773 | After 1776 |

B. Write questions of CHRONOLOGICAL ORDER.

What happened after _____ ?   How many years _____ ?
What happened before _____ ?   Between (*date*) and (*date*) who _____ ?
How long after _____ ?   Between (*date*) and (*date*) what _____ ?
How long before _____ ?   Between (*date*) and (*date*) how _____ ?
When _____ ?   Since 1773 _____ ?

C. This selection involves GEOGRAPHICAL information as well as CHRONO-
LOGICAL relationships.

Write sentences to answer the following questions:

1. Where did the officials who were supported by American taxes come
from?
2. In what place did the colonists act against the British company's
monopoly?
3. Where were the colonies' laws made?
4. From what direction did the colonies' tea come?
5. Where did the colonists throw the tea?
6. Across what ocean did the British company's ships sail?
7. Into what country was tea smuggled?

D. Look again at the questions in C. For which questions can you find EXPLICIT
answers? For which questions are the answers IMPLIED? Indicate which were
EXPLICIT and which IMPLICIT.

4. Chronological Order (Biography)

Listen to the following information about Lincoln.

1. When Lincoln was eight years old, his father lost most of his land in Kentucky.
2. Lincoln's mother died when he was nine years old.
3. Lincoln's stepmother persuaded his father that Abraham should begin to go
to school.
4. Lincoln was born in Kentucky.
5. He started school, but it soon closed.
6. The first winter they spent in Indiana they lived in a house with only three
walls; the fourth side was open for a fire.
7. Lincoln was born on February 12, 1809.
8. A little more than a year later Lincoln's father married again.
9. Lincoln's family moved to Indiana from Kentucky.
10. Two years later Abraham went for a few weeks to another school.

A. The information about Lincoln above is not in logical chronological order. Read
the sentences quickly to decide the order the sentences should follow.

B. Decide if any of the sentences can be COMBINED to make one sentence.

C. Write a paragraph about Lincoln in which you include all the information given
in the correct CHRONOLOGICAL ORDER.

BEFORE YOU WRITE:

A. RECALL IN ENGLISH what the exercise is about.
    REPEAT IN YOUR MIND the CONTENT information.
    REPEAT IN YOUR MIND the CONTENT vocabulary.

B. RECALL IN ENGLISH the method of written organization of the
    exercise.
    REPEAT IN YOUR MIND the STRUCTURE vocabulary.

WHILE YOU ARE WRITING:

A. DO NOT RELY ON COPYING. RETAIN in your mind what you are
    writing about and how it is to be written. Refer to the text only to
    refresh your memory.

B. ASK YOURSELF QUESTIONS while you write about the CONTENT
    and about the METHOD.

Introducing Spatial Order

Read silently while your teacher reads aloud.

Throughout this textbook you will learn a number of basic logical methods of organization. One of these is the arrangement of information according to PLACE or RELATIONSHIP in SPACE. In this text this kind of logical order is called SPATIAL ORDER. Very frequently SPATIAL ORDER and CHRONOLOGICAL ORDER go together.

A. Here is a diagram of a room.

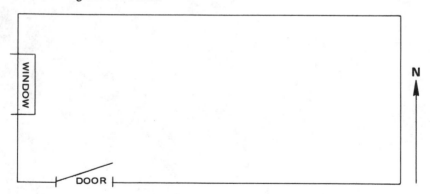

Add the following items to the diagram:

1. There is a sofa on the east wall facing the window.
2. There is a TV to the right of the door as you enter the room.
3. There is a coffee table in front of the sofa.
4. There is a desk in the middle of the north wall facing the door.
5. There is a bookcase beside the desk near the window.

B. Here is a diagram of another room. Write five statements of SPATIAL ORDER which are TRUE about the items in the room. (You may choose any you wish.)

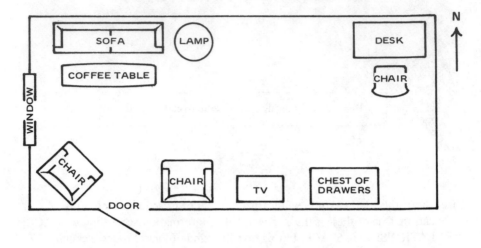

C. Write three statements of SPATIAL ORDER which are FALSE about the items in the room. (You may choose any you wish.)

Structure Vocabulary

The following is a list of *some* of the structure vocabulary you need when you write about spatial relationships.

You will use words like:

> where
> in which, to which, from which, etc.
> under, over, inside, beside, on top of, etc.
> along, through, as far as, etc.
> north, northern, south, southern, etc.
> to the left, to the right, to the north, etc.
> in back, in front, in the middle, etc.

Additional Space Order Vocabulary

adjacent	parallel	rectangle
corresponding to	parallel to	semicircle
distance	perpendicular to	slope
midpoint	plane	space
endpoint	opposite	surface
interior	overlapping	vertical
diagonal	pyramid	horizontal
edge	exterior	
limit	intersection	

Composition Exercises

5. Sentences Expressing Spatial Order

Write statements of SPATIAL ORDER to fit the following patterns. (You may need more than one word for each blank space.)

1. There is a _____ in front of _____ in my room.
2. Students should sign their name _____ their composition papers.
3. You can drive your car _____ the bridge.
4. On the dining-room table you usually find a knife _____ your plate and a fork _____ .
5. Michigan is in the _____ part of the U.S. while Florida is in _____ .
6. I never sit at the _____ of the auditorium or in the _____ because I like to sit _____ where the teacher won't notice me.
7. If you don't go to the right or to the left, you will _____ .
8. The roof is _____ the house.
9. I live _____ 312 Main Street _____ small town, but my friend lives _____ Johnson Avenue.
10. Never throw large balls _____ glass windows.

6. Chronological Order and Spatial Order (Map)

Examine the following map and the timetable of Mr. Jones's activities yesterday.

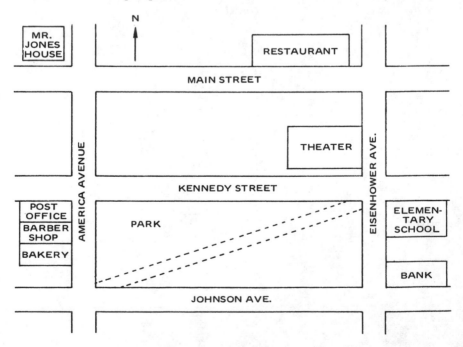

9 a.m.	ate breakfast	1:15-1:30	fed bread to the birds
9:30	took his child to school		in the park
9:45	had a haircut	1:30-4:30	worked in the bank
10-11:45	worked in the bank	4:40	bought theater tickets
noon	ate lunch in the restaurant	4:50	drank coffee in the
1 p.m.	bought stamps		restaurant
1:15	bought bread	5:30	arrived home

Note: Mr. Jones did not drive his car.

A. Write a summary of what Mr. Jones did yesterday, giving specific details about where he walked (i.e., along what street, etc.) and what he did. Do not omit anything. Use the past tense. Ask your teacher for help with prepositions of place and time if you need help.

B. From the information you have been given, make an INFERENCE about each of the following:

1. Mr. Jones's work.
2. Mr. Jones's family.
3. The restaurant on Main Street.
4. Mr. Jones's wife.

C. Examine the inferences you made. Decide where each of your inferences fits on this relative scale.

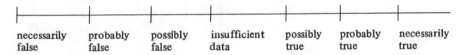

| necessarily false | probably false | possibly false | insufficient data | possibly true | probably true | necessarily true |

7. Spatial Order (Description)

Write a paragraph in which you use these details. Before you write, arrange the details to achieve SPACE ORDER. Decide where you are standing.

1. A green and white house on a corner.
2. A red car close to a telephone pole.
3. A man standing on the front steps of the house.
4. A second telephone pole on the corner of the street beside a pine tree.
5. A second tall pine tree in the back yard of the house.
6. A snow man on the lawn of the house.
7. A woman getting out of the red car.

You may want to draw a diagram before you start writing. There are several possible SPATIAL arrangements.

53

8. Chronological Order: Precise and Vague

Listen to the following information about silk.

About 4,000 years ago the Chinese learned how to unwind the cocoons made by silk worms in order to get the silk thread to make into cloth.

Nobody knows how this discovery came about. One story tells that one day around 2700 B.C. a silk cocoon fell into a hot cup of tea which a princess was drinking. When she tried to pick it out, she pulled out a long single thread of silk.

For hundreds of years the Chinese made silk cloth. They sold it to people in other countries but kept secret the process by which they made it.

A. Using the information you have read about silk, fill in the following chronological chart to answer the questions:

  1. When was silk discovered?
  2. When did the Chinese sell silk?
  3. When did other countries learn how to make silk?

3000 B.C.   1 A.D.   2000 A.D.

—————+——————————————————+——————————————————+—

B. Look again at the questions in A. For which of the questions can you find a definite answer in the passage? For which can you find only a VAGUE or IN-EXACT answer?

When we deal with CHRONOLOGICAL ORDER we sometimes cannot give a PRECISE, EXACT time. Then we use such phrases as

sometime before _____	it may be true that
sometime after _____	it might be true that
between _____ and _____	_____ may _____
before _____	_____ might _____
about _____	possibly
around _____	perhaps
it seems true that _____	as much as
it seems possible that _____	no more than
approximately	no less than
maybe	I hesitate to claim that _____

C. Write three CHRONOLOGICAL STATEMENTS that are VAGUE. You may choose any subject you wish.

D. Look again at the questions in A. For which questions did you need more information than the passage gives you? For which questions did you add information
from your own knowledge? In this book there are many composition exercises
in which you make INFERENCES. There also are many composition exercises
where you must contribute information that you know. (For example, that the
Chinese still make silk.) *Do not let your brain go to sleep! Use the information
you already know!*

9. Chronological Order and Spatial Order (Biography)

Listen to the following information about Kennedy.

1. When John Kennedy was at Harvard University, he injured his back playing
   football.
2. In August 1943 Kennedy's boat was destroyed when it was cut in half by a
   Japanese destroyer.
3. Kennedy graduated with honors.
4. Kennedy joined the Navy in 1942.
5. His back was reinjured when the two boats collided.
6. Kennedy graduated from Harvard in 1940.
7. Kennedy's back injury kept him out of the remainder of the war.
8. Kennedy swam for five hours to an island.
9. For many years Kennedy's back injury caused him pain.
10. While Kennedy was recovering from his operation, he wrote *Profiles
    in Courage.*
11. In 1954 Kennedy went to the hospital for a spinal operation.
12. His book won a prize for biography in 1957.

A. The information about Kennedy is not in order.

1. Look at the information for SPATIAL clues. In how many places does the
   biography take place? Arrange the information into SPATIAL categories;
   that is, group the sentences according to the question "where?"

2. Look at the information for CHRONOLOGICAL clues. Arrange the list you
   have made according to chronological order.

3. Decide if there are any sentences you can combine.

4. Write a paragraph about Kennedy, using the correct SPATIAL and CHRONO-
   LOGICAL order.

BEFORE YOU WRITE:

A.   RECALL IN ENGLISH what the exercise is about.
      REPEAT IN YOUR MIND the CONTENT information.
      REPEAT IN YOUR MIND the CONTENT vocabulary.

B.   RECALL IN ENGLISH the method of written organization of the
      exercise.
      REPEAT IN YOUR MIND the STRUCTURE vocabulary.

WHILE YOU ARE WRITING:

A.   DO NOT RELY ON COPYING. RETAIN in your mind what you are
      writing about and how it is to be written. Refer to the text only to
      refresh your memory.

B.   ASK YOURSELF QUESTIONS about the CONTENT, and about the
      METHOD.

B. Read again the information on Kennedy. What INFERENCE can you make about Kennedy's character from the paragraph? Write a sentence about his character. Do you consider your inference a FACT or an OPINION? Why?

C. Your paragraph about Kennedy is BIOGRAPHY. It is a BIOGRAPHICAL paragraph. Choose a famous person you know about. Write a paragraph of BIOGRAPHY about that person. Tell facts (not opinions) about him. Be sure they are in chronological order.

D. Write a sentence of INFERENCE about the character of the person you wrote about.

10. Chronological Order (Autobiography)

Read silently while your teacher reads aloud. "Repeat in your mind" what your teacher reads.

Many of the CHRONOLOGICAL ORDER exercises you have done have been BIOGRAPHICAL. Writing which is the biography of the writer is called AUTOBIOGRAPHICAL.

People are often asked to write about their own lives. Below is a list of words and phrases that can be used in an autobiographical paragraph.

1. First arrange the words and phrases in a sequential order.
2. Next choose the chronological clues you want to use.

3. Then write an AUTOBIOGRAPHICAL paragraph in which you use the time sequence you have chosen.

later	afterwards
before I attended school	before my *eighth* birthday
after I entered school	when I learned to read
next, subsequently	when I was born
when I was a child	finally
for _____ years	during my school vacations
while I was still learning _____	my *first* experience at school
while	when I was _____ years old
one day	as a _____ year old
one day while	

11. Chronological Order and Spatial Order (Biography)

Listen to the following information about Lindbergh.

1. In 1923 Charles Lindbergh made his first solo flight in Georgia.
2. Lindbergh tested his new plane for several weeks.
3. Charles Lindbergh was born in 1902.
4. At 7:15 p.m. on Friday, May 20th, Lindbergh passed over St. John's, Newfoundland.
5. At 8:00 a.m. on Saturday, May 21st, Lindbergh was 500 miles west of Ireland.
6. Lindbergh was born in Detroit, Michigan.
7. In 1927 Lindbergh got money from some businessmen in St. Louis to help build a special plane to fly across the Atlantic.
8. In 1927 he decided to try to fly alone from New York to Paris (3,600 miles).
9. Lindbergh flew so close to the surface of the ocean that he could see the waves in the moonlight.
10. Lindbergh won a $25,000 prize for the first non-stop flight from New York to Paris.
11. Lindbergh entered the University of Wisconsin in 1918 to study mechanical engineering.
12. Lindbergh flew northeast from New York.
13. Lindbergh called this new plane the Spirit of St. Louis.
14. Lindbergh landed in Paris at 5:21 p.m., Saturday, May 21, 1927 (10:21 p.m. Paris time).
15. Lindbergh passed the coast of Ireland around noon, Saturday, May 21st.
16. Lindbergh learned to drive a car when he was ten years old.
17. Lindbergh flew 1,900 miles across the Atlantic Ocean alone in the dark.
18. Lindbergh left the University to become a flier.
19. At 7:52 a.m. on Friday, May 20, 1927, Lindbergh left New York alone in the Spirit of St. Louis.

A. Using the map and these sentences, write a composition about Lindbergh in logical order. Note that in some cases there may be two possible answers about order. (For example, #7 and #8.) Choose the order that is the most logical. Decide what sentences can be combined. Combine them. How many paragraphs do you think this material should have? Where would you make the paragraph divisions?

B. Reread your composition. It gives EXPLICIT information. There are FACTS that are not explicitly stated which we can figure out. For example we can figure out how long the trip took, how many miles per hour he flew at, how old he was, etc. Write four factual questions about the Lindbergh information for which the answers are not explicitly given.

C. We can INFER some things about Lindbergh's character from the information we have. Write three sentences of INFERENCE about his character.

D. Some people consider Lindbergh *brave*; some say he was *foolhardy*. Which is derogatory?

Notice that when we talk about miles per hour we are talking about FACTS. We can agree on facts. When we make an inference about a person's character, we are dealing with OPINIONS. When you are writing, do not expect the reader to be able to guess what your opinion is about a person's character. Be EXPLICIT.

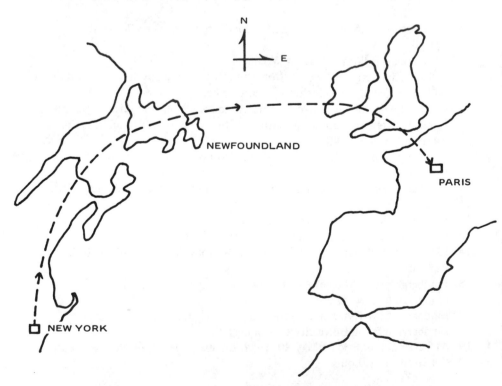

12. Chronological Order and Spatial Order (Murder Mystery)

Listen to the following information.

1. On January 3rd, 1968, it started to snow at 8:00 p.m.
2. At 10:00 p.m., January 3rd, 1968, someone called the police and said, "There's been a murder at the house on the corner of Grove Street and Johnson Avenue."
3. The first thing the police noticed was that the back door was open.
4. In the living room the police found the family of the murdered person.
5. The police found no footprints leaving the house.
6. Mr. Smith, Mrs. Smith, and her niece, Jane Jones, were in the living room.
7. The police came to the house ten minutes later.
8. Mr. Smith said, "My aunt has been killed. She is in her bedroom. The knife is lying on the bed beside her."
9. The policeman asked, "Who was in the house tonight?"
10. "I've been here all evening watching the TV," said Mr. Smith.
11. "I discovered the body when I went into the bedroom to show my aunt the new dress I bought tonight," said Mrs. Smith.
12. In the bedroom a policeman found the body of an old lady; she had been stabbed in the back.
13. "I was in my bedroom reading until 10:00 o'clock," said Jane.
14. Mrs. Smith said, "I went out shopping and didn't return until almost ten o'clock."
15. "We are very upset," sobbed Mrs. Smith. "We are the only relatives my aunt has."
16. On the floor beside the old lady was her empty jewel box.

A. The evidence you are given is not in logical order. Using time and space clues, arrange the information in logical order.

B. Write out three questions the police need to have answers to. Write them in question form.

C. Assume you are a detective. Add one piece of vital information to what you are given. This piece of information should help you decide who committed the murder. Write a sentence summarizing your extra piece of information.

D. Write a solution to the mystery. Your explanation should be in CHRONO-LOGICAL ORDER.

Content vocabulary you may want to use:

murder	coroner	inheritance	snowfall
murderer	autopsy	heirs	die
fingerprints	blood stains	victim	death
alibi	motive	stranger	crime
detective	inherit	outsider	criminal

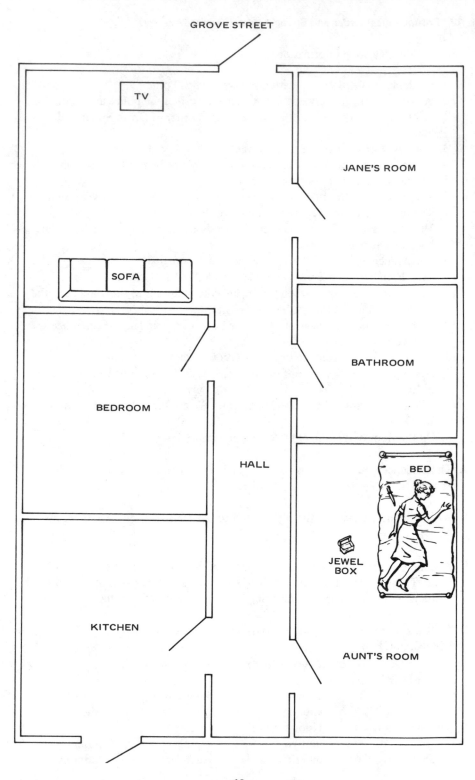

GROVE STREET

TV

JANE'S ROOM

SOFA

BATHROOM

BEDROOM

HALL

BED

JEWEL
BOX

AUNT'S ROOM

KITCHEN

13. Pronoun Reference: Review Exercise

All of these topics have appeared in previous exercises. Recall the content of the exercises. Recall the vocabulary.

What words did you substitute for the following to avoid being repetitious in your writing?

Charles Lindbergh	the President of the United States	the police
Lindbergh's plane	the U.S. Senate	businessmen
the United States	smoke	diseases
laws	pollution	smallpox
industries	the Supreme Court	the British
the Pony Express	Supreme Court Justices	independence
San Francisco	the weather	Kennedy's back injury
the Mayflower	food	a football team

14. Reverse Chronological Order (Communication)

All the following information is about communication. It is, however, not in the correct chronological order. Arrange the data in REVERSE CHRONOLOGICAL ORDER. Write a composition about communication in which you use this information.

You may add other data if you wish. Organize your material starting with what is most recent and work backwards to what is most remote in time. The following words and phrases can be used to express reverse chronological order.

prior to	since	origin of
earlier	previous	ultimate origin of
before	previously	ultimate source of
before that	derive from	ultimate beginning of
_____ ago	originate	

(number) (weeks, months, etc.)   before

1. The clipper ships transformed communication in the 1880's with speeds up to 360 nautical miles per day.
2. Marconi transmitted long-wave signals without wires in 1895 when he was only 21 years old. He laid the foundation for world-wide radio.
3. In antiquity, couriers were used to carry messages. In 490 B.C., a Greek runner is said to have run from Marathon to Athens, bringing news of victory. He died of overexertion after running 26 miles, 385 yards.
4. During the 18th and 19th centuries extensive use was made of signals using lanterns, flags and even moving arms to convey messages.
5. Horses were the swiftest carriers of news throughout most of history. A horse can run a mile in just over a minute and a half. Long distance runs of

over one hundred miles have been averaged by horses at 20 miles an hour.
6. Samuel Morse developed a telegraph system that would work long distance in 1837.

Content vocabulary you may want to use:

develop	speed
development	distance
growth	invent
evolution	invention

Introducing Generalizations and Specifics

Read silently while your teacher reads aloud.

Throughout this textbook you will learn a number of basic logical methods of organization. So far you have had practice in making inferences; that is to say, in drawing conclusions from data. Many of these inferences are GENERALIZATIONS. A generalization is a statement which has general application. A generalization is concerned with what is true or applicable in most instances. It is not limited in scope, and involves the obvious features, not the details. In writing it is necessary to *support* or *prove* generalizations by giving facts, examples, statistics, personal experiences, etc., so that the reader will be convinced that what you are saying is true.

For example, if you write:

Americans are materialistic people,

or

Astronauts are brave men,

the reader will expect you to support your idea by giving SPECIFIC DETAILS. SPECIFIC is the opposite of GENERAL.

Structure Vocabulary

The following is a list of *some* of the structure vocabulary you need when you support a generalization with specific details.

for example	in substantiation
for instance	to substantiate
for one thing	as an illustration
to illustrate	in one instance, in this instance
in one instance	as an example
in other words	take _____ , for example
as follows	consider _____ , for example
as proof	in practice
let me illustrate	according to statistics
let me cite as proof	according to statistical evidence

The following words and phrases are used for generalizations.

generally	all
generally speaking	every
on the whole	never
	always

63

Composition Exercises

15. Sentences Expressing Generalizations and Examples

Write STATEMENTS of GENERALIZATION and EXAMPLES to fit the following patterns.

1. Generally speaking, everybody likes _____ .
2. All students are _____ .
3. On the whole, _____ is a good place to live. For example, we can _____ there.
4. Doctors are _____ men. My doctor, for instance, always _____ .
5. I am always _____ . As proof, let me tell you about _____ .
6. Libraries are _____ places. Take, for example, _____ , where _____ .

Examine the sentences you have written. Which are GENERALIZATIONS? Which are EXAMPLES?

16. Generalizations and Specifics: Relevance

Good writers provide their readers with PROOF or with SUPPORTING DETAILS when they make generalizations. The supporting information must be RELEVANT. If the paragraph includes material irrelevant to the generalization, the reader will consider it illogical.

Relevant and Irrelevant Data

In a good paragraph of generalization, all the materials support the generalization. Find the IRRELEVANT material in the following:

A. Generalization:

The President of the United States has many powers.

Supporting Evidence:

1. The President can veto bills passed by the Congress.
2. The President appoints the members of the Supreme Court.
3. More Presidents have come from Virginia than from any other state.
4. The President is the Chief of the Cabinet.
5. The President is Commander-in-Chief of the armed forces.

B. Generalization:

Helen Keller was an exceptional woman.

Supporting Evidence:

1. Helen Keller became blind and deaf when she was an infant.
2. Helen Keller learned to read and write, and to speak.
3. Helen Keller died in 1968.
4. Helen Keller wrote many books.
5. Mark Twain said Helen Keller was one of the greatest persons who lived in this era.

C. Generalization:

Americans are very extravagant about their pets.

Supporting evidence:

1. In 1966 Americans spent $3 billion on dogs, dog food, and things for their dogs.
2. It is possible to find a psychiatrist, or a hairdresser for dogs in many U.S. cities.
3. The amount of money spent on pets in the U.S. is expanding at the rate of 30 percent per year.
4. Children should be taught to love animals.
5. A cook book for dogs tells how to feed dogs five-course meals.

17. Generalizations: Fact and Opinion

The generalizations we make can be either FACTS or OPINIONS. If we are dealing with a FACTUAL GENERALIZATION, we usually have no trouble convincing our readers of the logic of what we are saying. Facts can be checked and proved. When our generalization is an OPINION or a VALUE JUDGMENT, we cannot PROVE our idea. We can, however, write CONVINCINGLY about our opinion. We can choose good examples to support our opinion.

A. Which one of each of the following pairs of generalizations will be easier to PROVE or to WRITE CONVINCINGLY about?

1. (a)   The President has many powers.
   (b)   The President has too many powers.

2. (a)   Helen Keller was exceptional.
   (b)   Helen Keller was the most exceptional woman who ever lived.

3. (a)   Americans are extravagant about their pets.
   (b)   Americans are stupid and wasteful.

B. How can you make 1(b), 2(b) and 3(b) "easier" to write about? You can add:

> Some people (politicans, economists, etc.) think _____ .
> It is sometimes said _____ .

Write new sentences for 1(b), 2(b) and 3(b) in which the OPINIONS are QUALIFIED.

18. Generalizations and Specifics (U.S. History)

Listen to the following information about pioneer life in the United States.
1. The women did most of the doctoring and nursing.
2. Children often could not go to school; some were taught to read and write at home by their mothers.
3. Each member of the family shared the work.
4. The women, girls, and young children did the cooking, and made soap and candles.
5. Frequently the women of the family worked alongside the men in the fields.
6. All the family's clothing was made in the home.
7. The cabin was usually built close to a stream because it was dangerous for the mother and children to have to go far into the forest for water.
8. When the father was away from the cabin hunting, the mother always kept a rifle close at hand in case of Indian attack.

A. On the basis of this information, make a GENERALIZATION about pioneer life in the United States.

B. Is your GENERALIZATION a FACT or an OPINION?

C. Write a paragraph using the following organization.

Facts
Generalization (inference from facts)

Some content vocabulary you may want to use:

cooperate	independent	hardworking
cooperative	independence	close-knit
self-sufficient	indispensable	industrious

19. Generalizations and Specifics (U.S. Mobility)

Listen to the following information about mobility in the U.S.

1. Every year since 1950, twenty percent of U.S. families have moved to a different place.
2. In 1968, 41.5 million Americans moved to a different place of residence.
3. Many Americans save the boxes that toasters, clocks, and so on, come in so that they can pack them for moving more easily.
4. There are 3.5 million miles of highway in the United States.
5. The typical U.S. family stays in the same house 6½ years.
6. Fifty percent of the U.S. population does not live in its native state or native hometown.
7. Eighty-seven percent of U.S. adults have moved at least once since they became adults.
8. Six percent of the U.S. population moves at least 150 miles every five years.

A. On the basis of this information make a GENERALIZATION about people who live in the U.S.A.

B. Examine the data you are given. Is this information FACT or OPINION?

C. Is your generalization FACT or OPINION? Where would you place your generalization on this relative scale?

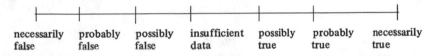

| necessarily false | probably false | possibly false | insufficient data | possibly true | probably true | necessarily true |

D. Write a paragraph using the following organization. Use only relevant data in your paragraph.

> Generalization (inference from facts)
>
> Facts (arranged in logical order)

Some content vocabulary you may want to use:

mobile	often
mobility	usually
moving industry	is used to ____ ing
moving company	frequently
moving van	statistics
movement	statistical

20. Generalizations and Specifics (Occupations)

A. Write five short (3 or 4 sentences) paragraphs of generalization and specific details about any of the occupations listed below. Use the following organization:

```
┌─────────────────────────────────────┐
│                                     │
│         General Statement           │
│                                     │
├─────────────────────────────────────┤
│                                     │
│       Relevant Specific Details     │
│                                     │
└─────────────────────────────────────┘
```

Your generalization should deal with the _____'s character or _____'s training.

B. After you have written your paragraphs, decide whether your generalizations are FACTS or OPINIONS.

For example:
Most airline stewardesses are beautiful.
Engineers should be mechanical.
Dancers are usually athletic.

Be sure to *exclude* all IRRELEVANT details from your paragraph. To be convincing your details must support your GENERALIZATION. RECALL vocabulary that you can use from earlier exercises.

Occupations

politician	singer	judge
doctor	dancer	executioner
nurse	soldier	priest, minister
teacher	policeman	dentist
astronaut	director	airline stewardess
historian	movie star	king
factory worker	dictator	student
racing car driver	clown	janitor
poet	animal trainer	athlete
engineer	explorer	salesman
dramatist	artist	
choreographer	musician	

21. Generalizations and Specifics (Autobiography)

There are many different kinds of specific details that can be used to support a GENERALIZATION. One kind that is frequently used is a biographical or autobiographical ANECDOTE. This kind of supporting detail is not really a *proof* of the generalization, but if it is well-chosen it can be a convincing support of a generalization.

A. Write a paragraph in which you support your opening sentence with a personal ANECDOTE.

> Opening sentence: I think I am a very _____ person.

> RECALL content vocabulary about personal characteristics from earlier exercises. Ask your teacher for other vocabulary you may need.

B. Do you think you are an optimist or a pessimist? Write a paragraph in which you tell about an experience in your life when you have behaved like an optimist or like a pessimist. Your paragraph will be an AUTOBIOGRAPHICAL paragraph. Start with a GENERALIZATION about your optimism or pessimism.

C. Because each person is different, we all react in different ways to different things and ideas. For example, some people hate detective stories and some people are terrified of high places, or dogs, or snakes. Choose one thing that you really dislike or fear.

Write an AUTOBIOGRAPHICAL paragraph in which you start with a GENERALIZATION about your fear or dislike.

D. Do you think you are a self-sufficient person? Write a paragraph in which you tell whether you think you are self-sufficient or not. Your paragraph will be AUTOBIOGRAPHICAL. Start with a generalization; then give autobiographical examples to support your opinion.

Content vocabulary you may want to use:

dislike (verb)	self confidence	optimist
dislike of	have confidence in	pessimist
afraid of	lack of confidence	optimistic
fear (verb)	satisfy	pessimistic
fear (noun)	satisfaction	indifferent to
fright	satisfied with	able
frightened of	fearful of	ability
frightened by	optimism	capable of ____ ing
confidence	pessimism	

22. Generalizations and Specifics (Occupations)

We have seen that two people do not always agree when they are asked to give an opinion about a person's character even though they are each told the same facts. To some people Columbus was stubborn; to others he seemed persistent.

A. Write a paragraph in which you describe one morning in the life of a person who has one outstanding characteristic:

a housewife who is *lazy*
a doctor who is *busy*
a *nervous* student before examinations
an airplane pilot who is _____
a small boy who is _____

Be sure to indicate specific time order. Write your paragraph in the past tense. Start your paragraph with a generalization about the person's character. Be sure that all the facts you give *substantiate* (prove) your general statement.

Introducing Classification

Read silently while your teacher reads aloud.

Throughout this textbook you will learn a number of basic logical methods of organization. One major logical method of organization is CLASSIFICATION: the grouping of items or data according to their similarities and differences. Some data can be classified in only one way, but most data can be classified in many different ways.

A. Consider the following items:

bread	meat	lettuce
milk	potatoes	soup
eggs	ice cream	pie

How many different methods of classification can be used for these items?

They can be classified according to food value, according to the time of day at which they are usually eaten, according to price, etc.

When you classify data, choose the kind (or kinds) of classification that seems most logical to you.

B. The following are denominations of U.S. money. Group them into two categories.

5¢	1¢
$5.00	$1.00
50¢	25¢
10¢	$20.00
$10.00	

How did you group them? Into what two classes of money did you divide them? Are there other ways of classifying them?

Complete the following sentence:

United States money can be divided into two kinds according to _____ .

71

C. Examine the following list. Divide the items in the list into two categories. Give a name to each of the categories.

a painting	a stamp	an opera
a television set	a bridge	a tape recorder
a piece of ceramics	a statue	a light bulb
a drama	a coin	

D. Explain why you divided the data as you did. Are there other ways to group the items?

The items you were given were a list, an ENUMERATION.

When we CLASSIFY, we group items in a list according to some kind of ORDER. There are usually several ways to CLASSIFY a list.

E. Mr. Smith thinks he is a remarkably fine person. He likes to tell people about his virtues. Here are some of the things he says about himself.

1. I don't smoke to excess.
2. I never beat my wife.
3. I donate money to charity.
4. I am pleasant to my fellow employees.
5. I've never stolen any money or cheated on my income tax.
6. I love my children and provide a good home and education for them.

Classify Mr. Smith's virtues.

Content vocabulary you may want to use:

positive	spiritual
negative	psychological
social	material
personal	materialistic

F. Examine the following English words. Divide them into groups. You can have as many groups as you wish. Be prepared to explain why you grouped them as you did.

stupid	eat	hope
athlete	philosophy	doctor
nurse	thin	introduce
think	biology	mathematics
beautiful	economist	mother

The data you are given are in no particular order. They are a list, an ENUMERA-TION. When we ENUMERATE, we merely list; when we CLASSIFY, we impose ORDER on a list.

72

Structure Vocabulary

Repeat the pronunciation of words and phrases after your teacher.

The following is a list of *some* of the structure vocabulary you need when you write about classification.

main kinds of	unimportant	clearly distinguishable
major kinds of	insignificant	easily distinguished
basic kinds of	similar	uncontestable differences
fundamental	dissimilar	uncontestable similarities
significant	contradictory	classify
important	opposing	divide
primary, secondary	opposite	
minor	contrasting	

Also words like:

kinds	types	attributes
methods	sources	characteristics
parts	regions	factors
divisions	origins	eras
categories	bases	times
classes	qualities	
classifications	aspects	

Phrases like:

mutually exclusive
according to _____
with respect to _____
_____ falls into _____ categories
_____ can be divided into _____ classes

Composition Exercises

23. Sentences Expressing Classification

Choose from the following list the appropriate word or word group which will complete these statements of CLASSIFICATION.

important attributes	classify
divide, divided	factors
mutually exclusive categories	types
clearly distinguishable eras	main types
major regions	major

1. I have visited two of the _____ of the United States.
2. The person I marry must have several _____ .
3. The history of my country falls into two _____ .
4. Biologists _____ living things into _____ .
5. Presidents can be _____ into several _____ according to their _____ achievements.
6. Many _____ enter into an important legal decision.
7. For good nutrition we should eat four _____ of food daily.

24. Classification (Communication)

Before we can write a composition of classification, we must
1) accumulate data
2) arrange the data into categories according to a logical method
3) eliminate irrelevancies.

A. Add data to the following list, i.e., ENUMERATE examples.

Methods of Communication

1. telephone	6. television	11.
2. teletype	7. smoke signal	12.
3. drum	8. voice	13.
4. newspaper	9. flags	14.
5. letter	10.	15.

B. Arrange the data into categories according to different ways of classification.

1st possible method of grouping: by efficiency
2nd possible method of grouping:
3rd possible method of grouping:

C. Write a composition using one method of classification. Be sure to eliminate any irrelevancies before you write.

Use one of the following suggested opening sentences:

1. We can divide communication into _____ basic kinds according to who uses it.

or

2. Communication falls into _____ classes according to _____ .

or

3. If we examine different kinds of communication, we can see there are different levels of efficiency.

Content vocabulary you may want to use:

auditory	economy of effort	kind of audience
visual	distribution	person to person
ancient	prevalence	invent
modern	common	invention
technical	uncommon	instinct
personal	kind of user	instinctive

25. Classification (Transportation)

Before we can write a composition of classification, we must
   1) accumulate data
   2) arrange the data into categories according to a logical method
   3) eliminate irrelevancies.

A. Add data to the following list, i.e., ENUMERATE more examples.

Methods of Transportation

1. steamship	6. horse	11.
2. sailboat	7. jet plane	12.
3. bicycle	8. bus	13.
4. canoe	9. train	14.
5. automobile	10. propeller plane	15.

B. Arrange the categories according to different methods of grouping.

> 1st possible method of grouping: by kind of power used
> 2nd possible method of grouping:
> 3rd possible method of grouping:

75

C. Write a composition using one method of classification. The following are suggested opening sentences.

  1. We can divide transportation into _____ major classes according to _____ .

or

  2. Transportation falls into _____ types in accordance with _____ .

or

  3. If we examine different kinds of transportation, we can see _____ different levels of _____ .

Content vocabulary you may want to use:

power	land	mass transport
efficiency	air	individual transport
distance	ease	convenience
long-distance	cost	technology
passengers	maintenance	historical development
sea	replacement	

26. Generalization and Classification

A statement of CLASSIFICATION is a kind of GENERALIZATION. Not all generalizations, however, are classifications.

A. Examine the following sentences and divide them into two kinds:

simple generalizations
generalizations which are classifications

  1. Americans are mobile people.
  2. U.S. pioneer farmers fall into two distinct classifications.
  3. There were two major sources of the U.S. population in the 19th century.
  4. The American character was influenced by the frontier.
  5. The U.S. expanded territorially by three methods.
  6. U.S. frontiersmen can be divided into three types.
  7. The U.S. territorial frontier disappeared in 1890 when there no longer existed a dividing line between settled and unsettled parts of the United States.
  8. Many aspects of the American character can be attributed to the American frontier.
  9. The civilization which developed in the United States differed from that of Europe.
  10. A number of foreign countries were directly involved in U.S. territorial expansion.

11. United States history as reflected by the concentration of people in cities can be divided into two clearly distinguishable periods.
12. The United States acquired two major regions from Mexico.

B. Are there any that could possibly be both? For example, how do you decide about 10? 7?

27. Classification and Chronological Order (U.S. History)

Listen to the following information which explains the maps of United States Territorial Expansion. The material is not in chronological order. The material is not in geographical (spatial) order.

A. Using the map and the written information, write a CHRONOLOGICAL SUMMARY of U.S. expansion. You do not need to use the sentences as they are stated. You may PARAPHRASE if you wish.

1. In 1819 Florida was purchased from Spain.
2. In 1846 Britain gave up its claims to the areas in the Northwest known as the Oregon Country. For a time it seemed that a war might be fought about the territory.
3. The U.S. acquired most of the land between the Appalachians and the Mississippi River by treaty with Britain in 1783. This area was later divided into the states of Ohio, Indiana, Illinois, Michigan, Wisconsin, Kentucky, Tennessee, Mississippi, and Alabama.
4. In 1776 the thirteen original colonies became the United States of America.
5. The Gadsden Purchase of a piece of land in the Southwest took place in 1853.
6. In 1803 the United States bought from Napoleon the Louisiana territory in what is called the Louisiana Purchase. The United States paid $15,000,000 for the territory, which is four times the size of France.
7. As a result of the war with Mexico, the United States gained land in the West by the Mexican Cession in 1848.
8. In 1845 Texas, which had originally belonged to Spain and had later become an independent republic, joined the United States. Its citizens voted to join the United States.

B. Writing Simple Classification

1. Using the maps of the U.S. Territorial Expansion, write questions using these patterns:

   How many kinds of _____ ?   How many eras _____ ?
   How many parts of _____ ?   How many regions _____ ?
   How many divisions _____ ?   How many methods _____ ?
   How many sources _____ ?

The answers to these questions are general statements of CLASSIFICATION.

2. Write brief paragraphs starting with each of the following sentences.

   (a)   The U.S. acquired territory by _____ methods.
   (b)   _____ countries were involved in U.S. territorial expansion.

   Use the following organization:

Sentence of classification
Supporting data (must have same number of parts as mentioned in opening sentence.)

   Content vocabulary you may wish to use:

extension	cession	acquisition	expansion
extend	cede	acquire	expand

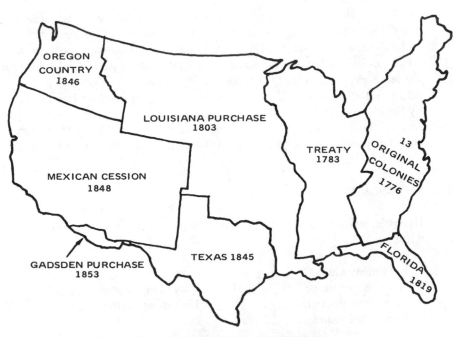

U.S. TERRITORIAL EXPANSION

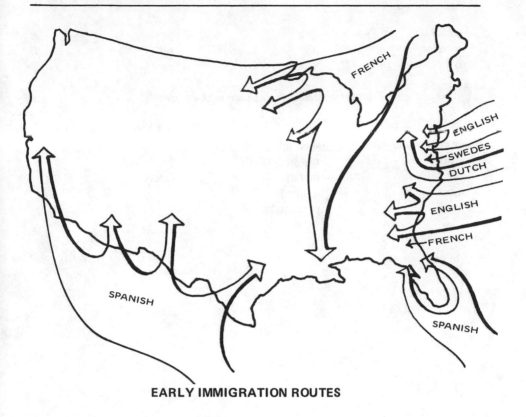

EARLY IMMIGRATION ROUTES

28. Classification (Economics/Geography)

A. Examine the following ENUMERATION of some of the principal products of North America. CLASSIFY the products into categories.

B. Write a composition about the products of North America. Use one of the following suggested opening sentences.

The principal products of North America fall into _____ .

or

In North America there are _____ major categories of products.

or

We can divide the products of North America into _____ with respect to _____ .

Products

corn	copper	dairy products
lumber	furs	grains (other than wheat)
cotton	silver	fish

cattle	iron	gold
tobacco	pigs	oil
fruit	wheat	coal

Content vocabulary you may wish to use:

plant products	crops	industrial necessities
animal products	seafood	fuel
fruit	raw materials	fossil fuel
vegetables	metals	fibers
citrus fruit	minerals	
grain	precious metals	

Introducing Comparison and Contrast

Read silently while your teacher reads aloud.

Another major logical method of organizing written data is COMPARISON and CONTRAST. Actually this is really *TWO* methods, but they are so closely related that they are usually considered together as a pair. COMPARISON is a statement or estimate of likenesses and similarities, while CONTRAST deals with differences and dissimilarities. COMPARISON and CONTRAST are often found in the same composition. Often in writing comparison and contrast it is necessary to make a SYNTHESIS, that is, to combine information from more than one source.

When we COMPARE, we talk or write about SIMILARITIES; when we CONTRAST, we talk or write about DIFFERENCES.

A. Read the following sentences and indicate if they are

> statements of CONTRAST
> statements of COMPARISON
> questions of CONTRAST
> questions of COMPARISON.

1. In what way was Kennedy's education different from Lincoln's education?
2. Jenner and Pasteur are both famous for their work in immunization.
3. The ball used to play softball is larger than a baseball.
4. The invention of the telegraph revolutionized communication as did the invention of TV later.
5. How is a drum similar to a telephone?
6. The United States purchased Florida from Spain; on the other hand, land in the west was acquired as a result of war.
7. Are you less of a pessimist than your father?
8. Today Americans are mobile just as the early pioneers were.

B. Consider the following information about two U.S. Presidents, Washington and Lincoln. Group the data into two classes: likenesses and differences.

1. Lincoln is credited with freeing the slaves.
2. Washington was a military man and a gentleman farmer.
3. As a farmer, Washington was a slave owner.
4. Lincoln's early life was marked by poverty.
5. Lincoln was President during the U.S. Civil War.
6. Washington was the fourth son of a rich Virginia family.

81

7. At the end of the Revolutionary War, Washington became the first President of the United States.
8. Lincoln was trained as a lawyer.

C. Write two questions of CONTRAST about Washington and Lincoln.

D. Write two questions of COMPARISON about Washington and Lincoln.

E. Write two statements of CONTRAST about the two Presidents.

F. Write two statements of COMPARISON about the two Presidents.

Structure Vocabulary

To Compare:	similar to	at the same rate as
	similarly	as
	like, alike	just as
	likewise	in like manner
	correspond to	in the same way
	correspondingly	to have _____ in common
	resemble	common *characteristics*, etc.
	resemblance	to be parallel in _____
	almost the same as	

To Contrast:	differ from	unlike
	however	in contrast (to)
	otherwise	in opposition (to)
	still	on the contrary
	nevertheless	on the opposite side
	even so	on the other hand
	dissimilarly	a larger percentage than
	different from	a smaller percentage than
	less than	at a different rate from
	more than	although
	faster than, etc.	while

Composition Exercises

29. Questions of Contrast

Write questions of CONTRAST using the following patterns. Choose any topic you wish.

1. How is _____ different from _____?
2. How does _____ differ from _____?
3. In what ways do _____ and _____ differ?
4. In what ways are _____ and _____ different?
5. What is the difference between _____ and _____?
6. What is the difference with respect to _____ between _____ and _____?

30. Sentences Expressing Contrast

Write statements of CONTRAST to fit the following patterns. (You may need a word or a phrase to complete the sentence.)

1. Lincoln's youth was _____ to _____ economically.
2. Some children grow _____ from other children because of nutritional differences.
3. _____ which is invisible is _____ smoke from coal.
4. The powers of the President _____ those of Congress.
5. As a child, Edison did not seem to be brillant; _____ people were impressed by him as an adult.
6. Before 1880 many people died of smallpox; _____ the percentage of deaths from smallpox is small today.
7. TV and newspapers are _____ in many ways even though their aims may be the same.
8. Jet planes are _____ the plane Lindbergh flew.
9. The _____ George III and Lord North can be seen in their _____ attitudes to the colonies.
10. Sound travels _____ through _____ than through _____.

31. Sentences Expressing Comparison

A. Write statements of COMPARISON to fit the following patterns. (You may need a word or a phrase to complete the sentence.)

1. _____ Supreme Court Justices, members of the Cabinet, are _____ by the President.

83

2. Florida and Louisiana have aspects _____ ; _____ belonged to Spain and they were acquired by _____ means.

3. The development of transportation and the development of communication _____ in many ways.

4. A man's wife's mother is his _____ ; _____ his mother is his wife's _____ .

5. The Pony Express was replaced by the telegraph _____ ; the clipper ships were _____ .

B. Examine the statements you have written. They are TRUE statements of COMPARISON. Rewrite them to get FALSE statements of CONTRAST.

32. Comparison and Contrast (Transportation)

Examine the following data about supersonic planes.

	SST	Concorde	TU-144
Origin	U.S.	British-French	Russian
Maximum take-off weight	750,000 lb.	385,000 lb.	330,000 lb.
Passengers	298	128	120
Length	298 ft.	193 ft.	188 ft. 6"
Wing span	143 ft.	84 ft.	72 ft.
Cruising speed	1,786 m.p.h.	1,350 m.p.h.	1,550 m.p.h.

A. Write three questions of COMPARISON.

B. Write three questions of CONTRAST.

C. Write three statements of CONTRAST which are FALSE according to the data.

D. Write three statements of CONTRAST which are TRUE according to the data.

E. Write three statements for which you have INSUFFICIENT EVIDENCE.

F. Write five questions about supersonic planes that the data do not answer.

33. Comparison and Contrast (Transportation)

Henry Ford was not the first man to make an automobile, but he is credited with mass production of the automobile.

Examine the following data about the Model T Ford.

Year	Price	Number Produced (in round numbers)
1909	$950	10,500
1910	$780	18,500
1911	$690	34,500
1912	$600	78,500
1913	$550	170,000

A. Write three statements of CONTRAST which are TRUE.

B. Write one statement of COMPARISON which is FALSE.

C. Write one statement of COMPARISON which is TRUE.

D. Write one INFERENCE about Ford based on the data.

E. Write one INFERENCE about car manufacturing based on the data.

F. Use the INFERENCE you wrote for E as the opening GENERALIZATION of a short paragraph.

34. Comparison and Contrast (Education)

Examine the following figures. The statistics are based on estimates from the U.S. Office of Education for the academic year 1969-70. Repeat the pronunciation of key words after your teacher.

Educational Institutions in the U.S.

Elementary	88,556
Secondary	31,203
Universities, Colleges, and Junior Colleges	2,483
Total	122,242

Elementary School Students

Public	32,600,000
Non-public (Private and Parochial)	4,300,000
Total	36,900,000

Secondary School Students

Public High Schools	13,200,000
Non-public	1,400,000
Total	14,600,000

College and University Full and Part-Time Students Enrolled for Credit Toward Degrees

Public institutions	5,100,000
Non-public	2,000,000
Total	7,100,000
Total Students Enrolled	58,600,000

Teachers

Elementary School Teachers	
Public	1,099,000
Non-public	152,000
Secondary School Teachers	
Public	904,000
Non-public	88,000
College and University Teachers	
Public	334,000
Non-public	188,000
Total	2,775,000

Board Members

Local School Board Members	106,806
State Board Members	500
College and University Trustees	25,000
Total	132,306

Administrators and Supervisors

Superintendents of Schools	13,106
Principals and Supervisors	119,365
College and University Presidents	2,483
Other College Administrative and Service Staff	82,000
Total	216,954

Cost (in billions of dollars)

Current Expenditures and Interest
    Elementary and Secondary Schools
        Public $32.7
        Non-public 3.8
    Higher
        Public 12.0
        Non-public 7.7
Capital Outlay
    Elementary and Secondary Schools
        Public 4.9
        Non-public 0.6
    Higher
        Public 2.6
        Non-Public 0.4

          Total $64.7

A. Write ten questions about education in the United States which the statistics do not answer.

B. Write three statements of CONTRAST which are TRUE.

C. Write three statements of CONTRAST which are FALSE.

D. Write three statements of COMPARISON which are TRUE.

E. Write three statements for which you have INSUFFICIENT EVIDENCE.

F. Write three INFERENCES based on the data.

35. Contrast and Classification (Business/Economics)

Examine the following data from the Bureau of Labor Statistics. The figures apply to the New York area. The quantity and quality of each of the items in the two lists are identical.

A. Write a statement of CLASSIFICATION based on the data.

B. Using the data, write a paragraph with

  (a)   an opening statement of generalization which is a CLASSIFICATION
  (b)   substantiation using at least two categories of data. (For this you need to classify the data. Note that there may be more than one way to classify the data.)

C. Assume you are

   (a)   an economist
   (b)   a restaurant owner
   (c)   a farmer

Formulate for each of these occupations three questions about the data. Be sure to make your questions relevant to "your occupation."

Use direct speech pattern:

        Mr. X asked, " _____ ?"

Then rewrite as indirect speech:

        Mr. X asked what the price was last year.

Supermarket Prices			
1967		**1970**	
potatoes	$ .76	milk	$ .60
hamburger	.74	bread	.28
apples	.21	chicken	.47
lettuce	.24	cornflakes	.33
tomatoes	.48	potatoes	.82
rib roast	.88	apples	.23
orange juice	.31	hamburger	.85
bread	.26	lettuce	.43
eggs	.68	tomatoes	.59
milk	.54	rib roast	1.01
chicken	.40	orange juice	.41
cornflakes	.29	eggs	.86

Content vocabulary you may want to use:

rise	food value	goods
fall	nutrition	manufactured goods
cost	nutritional value	salary
cost of living	supply/demand	solution/solve
standard of living	inflation	avoid ____ ing
factory	deflation	in accordance with
farm	government control	demand
rate	cost of living	stable
rate of cost rise	commodities	stabilize prices
dairy	increase	stability
butcher	decrease	market
baker	increment	income
retail	reduce	expenditure
wholesale	reduction	spend

36. Comparison and Contrast (Geography)

Examine the following data about two mountainous regions. The first region is in Mexico; the second is in Iceland.

Mexican Mountain Region

Sea level to 3,000 feet	Palms and tropical vegetation
	15 persons per square mile
From 3,000 feet to 11,000 feet	Hardwoods, grain fields, some desert regions
	20 persons per square mile to 7,000 ft.
	130 persons per square mile from 7,000-10,000 feet
11,000 feet to 12,000 feet	Evergreen trees
12,000 feet to 15,000 feet	Little vegetation
Above 15,000 feet	Barren, snow covered

Icelandic Mountain Region

Sea level to 2,000 feet	Evergreens
	10 persons per square mile
2,000 feet to 3,000 feet	Little vegetation
	10 persons per square mile
Above 3,000 feet	Barren

A. Write two statements of COMPARISON about the mountainous areas of the two countries.

B. Write five statements of CONTRAST based on the data.

C. Write two INFERENCES based on the data.

D. Write a paragraph of CONTRAST about the vegetation and the population distribution of the two countries.

37. Generalization, Comparison, and Contrast (Population/U.S. History)

The following data are about U.S. population growth. The data are statistical. In these exercises you are expected to utilize more than one kind of STRUCTURE VOCABULARY.

U.S. Population

1800	5,308,483
1820	9,638,453
1840	17,069,453
1860	31,443,321
1880	50,115,783
1900	75,994,575
1920	105,710,620

In 1800 — 3% lived in cities of 10,000
In 1860 — 15% lived in cities of 10,000
In 1840 — 4 cities of over 100,000
In 1860 — 8 cities of over 100,000
In 1900 — 38 cities of 100,000 or more
In 1920 — 68 cities of 100,000 or more
In 1900 — 402 cities of 10,000 to 100,000
In 1920 — 684 cities of 10,000 to 100,000

Examine the statistics.

A. Write three FACTUAL QUESTIONS based on the statistics.

B. Write three statements about the rate of population growth which are true. You may want to use such phrases as

percentage of	rapid increase
doubled in size	shoot up; shot up
tripled in number	decline
phenomenal increase	rise in population
slow increase	

C. Write a statement which is true about the rural character of the U.S.

D. Write a true statement of CONTRAST.

E. Write a statement of OPINION for which you have INSUFFICIENT DATA.

F. What additional facts would you need to know in order to use your statement of opinion (E) as a good sentence of generalization?

G. Write two sentences which you could use as opening sentences for paragraphs if you had to confine yourself to these data for SUBSTANTIATION.

H. (a)   If you want to write a paragraph on the nineteenth century population growth, what data are irrelevant?
(b)   If you want to write about the pre-Civil War U.S., what data are relevant?

I. Write a short paragraph on U.S. population growth before the Civil War. Start with a GENERALIZATION. Use only RELEVANT data as substantiation.

J. Write a short paragraph on U.S. urban population growth for one decade. Be sure you find the relevant material first. It may be necessary to use calculations and approximations.

Content vocabulary you may want to use:

urban	round numbers	census
rural	rounding off numbers	proportion of
farm	statistics	population rise
much population	ratio	population decrease
many people	percentage	

38. Synthesis, Comparison, and Contrast (Population)

A. Examine the world population graphs. Write sentences using these expressions of COMPARISON and CONTRAST:

almost the same as	less than
different from	more than
a larger percentage than	at almost the same rate as
greater than	at a different rate from

B. Examine the U.S. population statistics and the world population graphs. Using *both*, write a summary of U.S. population growth. For this you will make a SYNTHESIS, that is, you will combine two sources. You will need to round off numbers. Assume North American population figures equal U.S. figures (approximately).

C. Write three statements of CONTRAST which are TRUE.

D. Write three statements of CONTRAST which are FALSE.

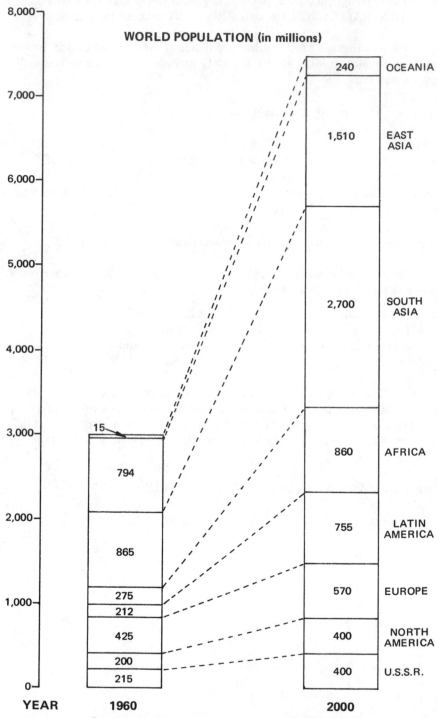

WORLD POPULATION (in millions)

	1960	2000	
	15	240	OCEANIA
	794	1,510	EAST ASIA
		2,700	SOUTH ASIA
	865	860	AFRICA
	275	755	LATIN AMERICA
	212	570	EUROPE
	425	400	NORTH AMERICA
	200	400	U.S.S.R.
	215		

YEAR   1960   2000

Based on *Population Bulletin,* vol. 21, no. 4, Oct. 1965.
Used with permission.

39. Comparison and Contrast (News Media)

A. Examine the following data.

1. In 1969 there were approximately 1,750 newspapers (written in English) in the United States.
2. There were 328 morning papers and 1,443 evening papers.
3. There were 578 Sunday papers.
4. The daily papers had a circulation of 62,500,000.
5. The Sunday papers had a circulation of around 49,500,000.
6. In 1960 there were 116 million home radios in the United States.
7. In 1960 there were about two million TV sets in the United States.
8. In 1968 there were 216 million home radios in the United States.
9. In 1968 there were 64½ million black and white TV sets and 20 million color TV sets.
10. The population of the United States in 1960 was 179 million; in 1969 it was 202,700,000.

B. On the basis of these data, write three TRUE statements of CONTRAST.

C. On the basis of these data, write three TRUE statements of COMPARISON.

D. Write a paragraph of COMPARISON and CONTRAST about the availability of news media to the U.S. population.

40. Generalization and Synthesis (U.S. Immigration)

Listen to the following information about U.S. immigration in the nineteenth century. The information is in CHRONOLOGICAL ORDER.

1. Many early settlers came to the U.S. to seek freedom: religious freedom, political freedom, and economic freedom.
2. In 1790 the first government census showed that 90% of the white population was British in origin (mainly English).
3. Up to 1820 approximately 5,000 people a year emigrated to the United States. By 1830 the number of immigrants per year was 20,000. In 1854, 428,000 people came to the United States from other countries.
4. In the 1840's there was a famine in Ireland. Many Irish emigrated to avoid starvation. They came to New York City and Boston to work in factories; many worked for the railway companies helping to construct railways.
5. In the 1840's the German revolutionary movement failed and many Germans emigrated to the United States.
6. In 1862 the Homestead Act was passed by Lincoln. Free land was offered to immigrants who became citizens. In 1864 a Commissioner of Immigration was appointed in Washington. His task was to spread information about the free lands to prospective immigrants.

7. After the 1849 gold rush, many Chinese immigrants came to the Pacific coast to work in mines and on railroad construction. In 30 years, opposition to Chinese immigration grew because of an unemployment problem in the United States. In 1880 there were anti-Chinese riots. In 1882 Chinese were barred from becoming U.S. citizens.

8. In the 1880's European farmers experienced an economic crisis when farm prices fell. During the 1880's 500,000 farmers a year came from Europe to the United States.

9. Until the 1880's immigrants came mainly from Northwest Europe. About 1882 there was a change in the character of immigration. Before 1882 immigrants from South and East Europe numbered 10% of the total. By 1890, 80% of the total number of immigrants came from South and East Europe and numbered one million yearly.

10. In 1882 the first restrictive immigration laws were passed. Convicts and idiots were not allowed to enter the United States.

11. In 1921 Congress passed a quota law which limited the number of immigrants from any European country to 3% of the nationality in the United States in 1910. The quotas restricted immigration from South and East Europe in favor of those from Northern Europe.

12. The 1924 law restricted the yearly total to 180,000 but in 1929 the total annual quota was reduced to 150,000 and excluded all orientals.

A. Writing Generalizations

1. From this information formulate three FACTUAL GENERALIZATIONS. Decide how you would substantiate these factual generalizations. Use one of the three as the opening sentence of a brief paragraph.

2. From this information formulate one INFERENCE which is DEROGATORY. Your inference will be an OPINION.

3. From this information formulate one INFERENCE which is FAVORABLE. Your inference will be an OPINION.

4. Choose one of the two inferences you have made. Write a paragraph using your inference. Choose your substantiating data very carefully. Be careful to include only relevant material which supports your opinion.

B. Examine the map "Major Routes of Early U.S. Immigration." Use the information from the map plus RELEVANT information from the immigration data to write a brief summary of the national groups who came to what is now the United States before 1880. Your SUMMARY will be a SYNTHESIS of the relevant information from the two sources. Before you write you will probably want to make a list of the information from the two sources.

C. Examine the maps which show U.S. territorial expansion. Using the maps and the information on immigration, make a list of all the information you have on the United States in the 1840's. Arrange the information in the list in logical order. Your list may be in CHRONOLOGICAL ORDER or your list may be according to CATEGORY (kinds of information). Write a paragraph about the United States in the 1840's organized according to one of these two methods.

D. Examine the statistics for U.S. population growth. In the immigration data we learn that the Homestead Act was passed in 1862. Using the information from both sources write a paragraph about the Homestead Act. Your opening sentence will be a GENERALIZATION about the Homestead Act. For example:

> The Homestead Act was extremely successful.
> The Homestead Act was moderately successful.
> The Homestead Act was a failure.

E. Using the U.S. population statistics and the immigration information assemble data to show the difference between the population of the United States in the 19th century (that is, up to around 1900) and after 1900. List your information. Examine the data to see if you can make any generalizations. Write a paragraph of generalization and substantiation of the difference between 19th century and early 20th century United States.

41. Writing Fact Questions: Review

A. Write questions based on the U.S. immigration and U.S. population growth data. Each question must fit the kind of answer indicated.

KIND OF ANSWER	QUESTION
Time	During which period did the U.S. population increase most rapidly?
Place	
Percentage	
Method	
Yes/No	
Contrast	
Number	
Name of Person	
Classification	

B. Write questions about the following topics. All the topics have been introduced in previous exercises. For each of your questions you are given the answer. Your question must fit the answer.

TOPIC	QUESTION	ANSWER
1. The Homestead Act	Who signed the Home-stead Act into law?	Lincoln.
2. transportation		3.5 thousand miles
3. pioneer life		Women.
4. birth of a U.S. President		Kentucky.
5. a useful discovery		Around 4,000 years ago.
6. U.S. territorial expansion		By war.
7. transportation		To win a $25,000 prize.

95

8. a crime	A snowy evening.
9. communication	Long wave signals without wires.
10. communication	By voice.
11. two U.S. Presidents	They both fought in wars.
12. transportation	It carries more passengers.
13. two U.S. Presidents	One was a lawyer, but the other was a farmer.
14. two famous inventors	They both were bad students in school.
15. immigration	By a quota law.

42. Writing Statements: Review

Write statements about the following topics. All the topics have been introduced in previous exercises. For each of your sentences you are told the kind of statement it must be.

TOPIC	STATEMENT	KIND OF STATEMENT
1. transportation of messages in ancient and modern times		CONTRAST which is TRUE
2. vaccines		CLASSIFICATION which is FALSE
3. origin of people living in the U.S.		CONTRAST which is TRUE
4. teachers		CLASSIFICATION which is TRUE
5. immunization		EXAMPLE
6. U.S. Presidents		GENERALIZATION which is FALSE
7. taxation of American Colonies		CHRONOLOGICAL ORDER which is TRUE
8. air pollution		GENERALIZATION which is TRUE
9. inventors		COMPARISON which is TRUE
10. extravagance		EXAMPLE
11. U.S. purchase of land		CHRONOLOGICAL ORDER which is FALSE
12. price increase		CONTRAST which is TRUE

Level Two Exercises

Instructions

> Read silently while your teacher reads aloud.

The exercises in this book increase in difficulty. Obviously, the first exercises which you have completed are easier than the later ones. In all the exercises you are asked to manipulate data. In the first exercises most of the data are provided, as is most of the vocabulary. In these next exercises you are asked to RECALL vocabulary from earlier exercises. You are asked to combine more than one METHOD of LOGICAL ORGANIZATION which means you must RECALL earlier STRUC-TURE VOCABULARY. You are asked to make more INFERENCES and AS-SOCIATIONS.

These are the instructions you are to follow for the next series of exercises.

BEFORE YOU WRITE:

A. RECALL in English the CONTENT information in this exercise. REPEAT in your mind the CONTENT information. REPEAT in your mind the CONTENT vocabulary.

B. RECALL in English the METHOD of written organization of this exercise. REPEAT in your mind the STRUCTURE vocabulary.

C. MAKE ASSOCIATIONS. TRY to RECALL other CONTENT ideas and vocabulary you can use from other exercises. TRY to RECALL STRUCTURE vocabulary you can use from other exercises.

D. THINK about INFERENCES and LOGICAL RELATIONSHIPS you can use based on this exercise and other exercises.

WHILE YOU ARE WRITING:

A. DO NOT RELY ON COPYING. Retain in your mind what you are writing about and how you are organizing your ideas. Refer to the text only to refresh your memory.

B. ASK YOURSELF QUESTIONS about

    CONTENT
    METHOD
    INFERENCES
    ASSOCIATIONS AND RELATIONSHIPS.

The instructions are enclosed in boxes. These instructions will appear in many of the exercises to help you remember the system you are to follow.

Composition Exercises

43. Comparison and Contrast (Exploration)

At the opening of the nineteenth century about four-fifths of the land area of the world was unexplored. By the end of the 19th century most of the land on earth had been explored. Early explorers suffered great hardships. More recent explorations have been made easier by modern inventions. Here are some of the inventions which have been of value to explorers:

> the radio
> the camera
> the airplane
> the helicopter.

A. Write five QUESTIONS of COMPARISON *or* CONTRAST about the differences and similarities of early and recent explorations.

B. Write a composition of COMPARISON and CONTRAST in which you tell the ways in which you think exploration today is like earlier explorations and also the ways in which you think present-day exploration is different.

Content vocabulary you may want to use:

danger	record	in contact with	baggage
unknown	supplies	weather	equipment
accident	disease	speed	route
communication	contact	transport	rescue

44. Comparison and Contrast (Sociology)

Write a composition in which you compare and contrast the self-sufficiency of the U.S. pioneers and the way of life of a modern American city-dweller. Before you write, try to RECALL vocabulary you will need. CLASSIFY the aspects of life you wish to discuss.

45. Classification and Synthesis (U.S. History/Population)

A. Refer to

   (a)   information on U.S. immigration
   (b)   statistics of U.S. population
   (c)   maps.

Using all three, formulate questions of CLASSIFICATION using these patterns:

How many major categories of _____ ?
How many main reasons for _____ ?
How many significant attitudes _____ ?
How many contrasting attitudes _____ ?
How many important sources of _____ ?
How many easily distinguished historical points _____ ?
How many similar aspects _____ ?
How many main methods _____ ?

B. Write a paragraph for which you can use the answer to one of the above questions as your opening sentence. Your paragraph will be a paragraph of CLASSIFICATION. It will have a generalization of CLASSIFICATION for the first sentence. For example:

The history of the U.S. as shown by _____ can be divided into periods. _____ important aspects of European life in _____ influenced the U.S. population.

Be sure your substantiating data are RELEVANT.

46. Comparison and Contrast (Biology)

During hot weather many people in the U.S. use electrical air conditioning. The efficiency of an air conditioner is measured in BTU's (British Thermal Units). One BTU equals the amount of heat required to raise the temperature of one pound of water one degree Fahrenheit. The average home air conditioner uses five thousand to seven thousand BTU's to cool a medium-sized room. Daily evaporation from a large tree cools the air, particularly if the tree is well-watered. The daily evaporation from a single tree can produce the effect of more than one million BTU's of an air conditioner.

A. Use the data to write sentences of COMPARISON and CONTRAST using the following phrases:

as important as	different from
less essential for	at a greater rate than
as vital as	more crucial for

B. What questions would you like to ask the writer of these data? Write four questions which should elicit additional information about the relative value of trees and air conditioners.

C. Write a composition about the values of trees and air conditioners. Use the data you are given. Make INFERENCES and ASSOCIATIONS. Draw on your own experience.

47. Comparison and Contrast (Government)

Use any relevant information you have been given in earlier exercises about U.S. government plus any of the following data which you consider relevant to write a composition in which you COMPARE and/or CONTRAST the government of the U.S. and the British parliamentary system. You should classify the aspects of government you wish to consider.

The information which follows is *randomly* arranged.

1. It is possible for a U.S. President to be of one major political party while the majority of senators and members of the House of Representatives belong to the opposing party.
2. The British Parliament has two houses, the House of Commons and the House of Lords.
3. Members of the House of Lords hold hereditary titles, are clergymen, or hold non-hereditary life peerages granted by the King or Queen for outstanding service.
4. The House of Commons has in excess of 600 members.
5. The House of Lords has about 875 members.
6. Members of the House of Commons are elected from districts; each district has about the same population.
7. General elections must be held every five years for all members of the House of Commons.
8. The King or Queen appoints as Prime Minister the leader of the party that has the most members in the newly elected House of Commons.
9. The Prime Minister chooses his cabinet.
10. The King or Queen has the right to veto laws but this right has not been used since 1714.
11. Cabinet members of the British government must be members of the House of Lords or House of Commons.
12. The House of Lords is not as powerful as the House of Commons.
13. The U.S. Supreme Court can declare a law unconstitutional.
14. Great Britain has no written constitution.

48. Writing Statements: Review Exercise

Write sentences using the following sentence patterns. Indicate for each sentence what *KIND* of statement you are making.

generalization	chronological order
example	spatial order
comparison	classification
contrast	

Use as many words as you need to complete your sentences.

Sentence Patterns

1. It is generally unfair to _____ .
2. The outstanding fact about _____ , when compared with _____ , is that _____ .
3. The most notable difference between _____ and _____ is _____ .
4. _____ major classes of _____ are present in _____ .
5. _____ , for instance, is based on _____ .
6. _____ and _____ differ in that _____ .
7. The task of _____ was first to _____ , then to _____ , and finally to _____ .
8. On the whole, _____ are acknowledged to be _____ .
9. Between _____ and _____ , there was _____ .
10. The difficulties the _____ experienced are exemplified by _____ .

49. Reverse Chronological Order (Communication/News Media)

In reverse chronological order the information is organized so that the writer starts with what is most recent and proceeds backwards to what is most remote in time.

The following information about newspapers is presented in random order.

A. Examine the data. Group the information into categories.

B. Write a composition about newspapers in which you use the data. Your composition will fall into sections according to CONTENT. You may include INFERENCES if you wish. CHRONOLOGICAL DATA must be presented in REVERSE order.

Listen to the following data:

1. The average annual income for U.S. newspapers was more than a billion dollars in the 1960's.
2. In 1875 a U.S. newspaper with a circulation of 50,000 was remarkable.
3. The number of newspapers in the U.S. has declined because of competition for circulation.
4. Three-fourths of newspaper income comes from advertising.
5. The highest number of daily newspapers ever published in the U.S. was 2,494.
6. In the 1960's one New York City newspaper sold over 2 million copies daily and more than 4 million on Sunday.
7. Weak newspapers are absorbed by their stronger rivals.
8. A newspaper chain is usually made up of several newspapers published in different cities but with the same owner.
9. The first daily paper in the U.S. was published in Philadelphia in 1774.
10. The first regular newspaper in England appeared in 1662.
11. All papers of a chain use the same feature articles, cartoons, comics, etc., but each one prints the city and state news in its territory.

12. In 1615 a newsletter was developed into the first regular weekly newspaper, the *German Frankfurter Journal.*
13. The Associated Press and the United Press International are two large news-gathering organizations.
14. During the Revolutionary War more than 30 papers appeared regularly in the U.S.
15. The first newspaper in the U.S. was published in Boston in 1690; it was suppressed by the British governor.
16. The Associated Press began in 1848 with six newspapers; it subsequently expanded to approximately 1,400.
17. In early times notices and bulletins were posted in public places.
18. The development of the telegraph and railroad increased the circulation of newspapers.

50. Classification (Education)

A small college in the Midwest is organized into eight major academic divisions. These are:

Language and Literature	Mathematics
Pure Science	Social Science
Applied Science	Physical Education
Music and Fine Arts	Journalism

A. The President of the college thinks that the eight major academic divisions should be reorganized. He is not sure how many divisions there should be and what they should include. You have been appointed to a committee to consider changes in the academic organization. Write a report in which you explain what major divisions you would advocate and why. Include in your proposals specific courses the divisions would include as well as general criteria for their inclusion.

B. The faculty of the college has proposed several new courses. Examine the title of each of the new courses and then write a one-sentence recommendation for each course for the major academic division in which it should be taught. Explain the reason for your choice.

New courses proposed

1. Introduction to Ceramics	6. Scuba Diving
2. The Philosophy of Aesthetics	7. Economics of Pollution Control
3. Law for the Layman	8. Introductory Anthropology
4. Introduction to Bibliographic Methods	9. Child Psychology
5. Ecology	10. Computer Language

C. The majority of freshmen who attend this small college are eighteen years old, have been educated in small-town high schools, and are intellectually relatively unsophisticated. According to the rules of the college all freshmen must take four required courses in their freshmen year. What four courses do you consider indispensable for these college freshmen? Explain your personal opinion; describe each of the courses you would make compulsory and tell why.

Content vocabulary you may want to use:

subject	special	interrelated	cooperate
department	specialist	succeed	cooperative
branch	specialize	success	autonomy
knowledge	profession	alternative	include
training	elementary	construct	inclusive
career	advanced	reconstruct	incorporate
literate	introductory	implement	incorporation
humanistic	confuse	implementation	handle
scientific	separate	independent	handled by
competent	relate	independence	contain
competence	related	interdependent	composed of
general	comprise	interdependence	

51. Writing Questions

A. Mr. A is a foreign student in the U.S. He wants to get a summer job working in the U.S. in order to earn money to pay for his tuition next year. He has an interview with the college foreign student adviser to get information about possible jobs. Write six questions he should ask. Use direct question form (e.g., Do I need to pay income tax if I work in the U.S.?) Indicate the kind of answer he expects to get.

Examples:

QUESTION	*KIND OF ANSWER*
Will I have to pay income tax?	Yes/No
Where is the nearest employment agency?	Place

B. Mr. B is applying for a position in an investment bank in New York City. He is worried about the interview he will have with the personnel manager, so he is trying to figure out ahead of time what kinds of questions he may be asked. Decide on six questions he should be prepared to answer. Write the questions in indirect form (e.g., The personnel manager will probably ask . . . . The personnel manager will want to know . . . .). Indicate the kind of answer he should be prepared to give.

Example:

QUESTION	*KIND OF ANSWER*
The personnel manager will want to know where he went to college.	Place

52. Classification, Comparison, and Contrast (Geography)

The following information is about two states: Arizona and Michigan. Utilize the following data to write a theme of comparison and contrast about Arizona and Michigan. You may not wish to use all the data. Before starting to write:

Group the data into categories for each state.
Find categories that compare.
Find categories that contrast.
Arrange the areas of comparison and contrast in order.
Write a generalization to include all areas of comparison and contrast.

Your composition will consist of a generalization of comparison and contrast, and SUBSTANTIATION of your generalization (use enumeration within each category to substantiate your generalization).

You should use vocabulary of comparison and contrast, and words like

former
latter
respectively

ARIZONA:

Population (1960)	1,302,161
Urban	74.5%
Rural	25.5%
Area	113,909 square miles
Temperature	
lowest	−33°F.
highest	127°F.
Land Use	2% crops
	62% pasture
	25% forest
	11% other

About 70% of the land is owned by the Federal Government.

Natural Resources
    copper (1st in the U.S. as a   zinc
        producer of copper)   asbestos
    gold   uranium
    lead

Arizona is 12th in the U.S. in mineral production.
The average value of Arizona's mineral production is 375 million dollars per year.

Arizona is 26th in the U.S. in lumber production.

Only 2% of total land in Arizona is harvested cropland. 90% of Arizona's agriculture depends on irrigation. Average farm size is 3,500 acres.

Products

cotton	lettuce
cattle	citrus fruits

Until after World War II Arizona's economy was based mainly on copper, cotton, cattle, citrus fruit, and its climate.

Because of its scenic beauties and its dry hot climate, Arizona has a thriving tourist trade. There are 30 Indian tribes in Arizona. The Grand Canyon is in Arizona. Tourists go to Arizona to ski, to ride, and to recover their health. Since World War II manufacturing has become an important economic factor in Arizona. Industries include food processing, aircraft, copper smelting, printing, and publishing.

MICHIGAN:

Population (1960)	7,823,194
Urban	73.4%
Rural	26.6%
Area	58,216 square miles (including 1,197 square miles of water surface)

Area of Great Lakes — 38,575 square miles (not included above)

Temperature

lowest	−51°F.
highest	112°F.

Natural Features

Lake Michigan and the Straits of Mackinac divide the state into 2 peninsulas.

Farm Products

Michigan has 150,000 + farms. Average farm size is 100 acres.

Michigan is the 5th state in manufacturing in the United States. The value of Michigan manufacturing is 8 times the value of its farming, mining, forestry and fishing combined.

More than 4 million tourists visit Michigan annually.

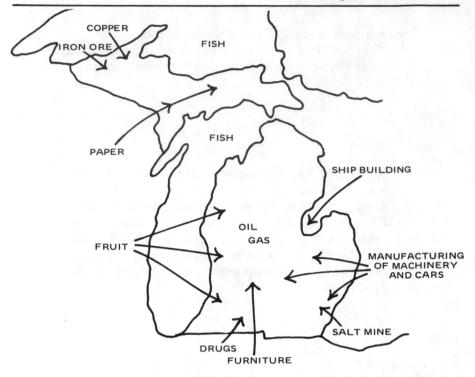

CROPS: APPLES   VACATION RESORTS: ON LAKES
                 CHERRIES   IN NORTH
                 PEACHES
                 POTATOES   20 STATE PARKS
                 SUGARBEETS
                 BEANS

Content vocabulary you may want to use:

the state of _____	resource	geography
product	wealth	geographic
manufacturing	source of income	scenery
manufactured product	recreation	scenic
industry	tourist	asset
industrial	tourism	produce
agriculture	facility	production
agricultural	harvest	export
mineral	crop	import
population density	topography	prosperity
distribution	per capita	prosperous

53. Writing Statements: Review Exercise

Use the following phrases to write sentences.

as important as	absolutely different from
more important than	unrelated to
less vital than	the reverse of
as essential as	mutually exclusive
less crucial for _____ than _____	superficially similar to

Indicate the *KIND of RELATIONSHIP* each of your sentences shows. Indicate the *TOPIC* of each sentence.

Introducing Classification by Expansion

Read silently while your teacher reads aloud.

When we CLASSIFY data, we divide the information into CATEGORIES. The categories may all be of equal importance, or may vary in importance. In one particular kind of classification, CLASSIFICATION by EXPANSION, the categories are of sequentially increasing importance or size. In CLASSIFICATION by EXPANSION the categories are arranged so that they form a hierarchy. For example, we might classify the place where we live according to this hierarchy:

> room
> apartment
> apartment building
> street
> city, etc.

Or we can classify laws according to this hierarchy:

> personal rules of conduct
> family rules
> municipal rules
> state rules
> federal rules

A. Complete a hierarchy of classification for each of the following:

   (1)   communication by voice
   (2)   communication by writing

B. Write a composition of CLASSIFICATION by EXPANSION about methods of communication in which *a personal letter* is one of the classes.

C. Write a composition of CLASSIFICATION by EXPANSION in which *a wheel* is one of the steps.

Composition Exercises

54. Classification by Expansion (Government/Business)

A. Write a composition about government in which you use CLASSIFICATION by EXPANSION as your method of organization. (Your hierarchy should have at least three steps.)

B. Write a composition about one of the following:

> business management
> food production and distribution
> banking
> advertising

Use CLASSIFICATION by EXPANSION as your method of organization. Be sure to give specific examples to illustrate each of the steps in your hierarchy.

55. Classification by Expansion (Travel)

Write a composition about travel in which you use CLASSIFICATION by EXPANSION as your method of organization. (Your hierarchy should have at least four steps.)

56. Classification by Expansion (Health/Sociology)

A. Write a composition about health and disease prevention in which you organize your ideas according to CLASSIFICATION by EXPANSION.

B. Write a composition about your place in society in which you organize your ideas according to an EXPANDING HIERARCHY.

Content vocabulary you may wish to use:

clean	facilities	infection
cleanliness	family	infectious
diet	familial	play a part in
nutrition	organization	cooperate with
rest	profession	cooperation
recreation	peer group	rights
public health	peers	responsibilities
personal	interact	duties
municipal	interaction	
society	communicable disease	

57. Comparison and Contrast (Geography)

The following data are about 2 countries: FINLAND and NEW ZEALAND.

A. 1. Write three questions of COMPARISON and CONTRAST for which you are given sufficient information.
   2. Write three questions of COMPARISON and CONTRAST for which you are *not* given sufficient information.
   3. Write two questions of CAUSE and EFFECT for which you are *not* given the answers.
   4. Write two statements of PREDICTION about the countries.
   5. Write two statements of PERSONAL OPINION about the countries.

B. Write a composition in which you compare and contrast the two countries according to:

   (a) population
   (b) geography
   (c) resources and industries
   (d) government

Remember that your composition should tell in what ways the two countries are alike and in what ways they are dissimilar.

FINLAND:

Area	130,119 square miles
Population (1968)	4,688,000

Finland is bordered by Sweden, Norway, and the USSR. The north has mountains 3,000-4,000 feet high; south and central Finland is flat. 70% of the land is forested.

Crops are oats, barley, wheat, rye, potatoes, and hay. The chief industry is associated with lumber. 60% of total exports are from wood, paper, and wood-pulp products. Other industries include shipbuilding, machinery, textiles, leather, and chemicals.

In 1968, 1,200,000 tourists visited Finland.

The government is a republic. There is one legislative chamber of two hundred members, elected to four-year terms. The President serves for six years. He is elected by three hundred members of an Electoral College. The electors are voted for by the people. The President appoints his cabinet. Finland is a member of the United Nations. The people speak Finnish or Swedish. There is no illiteracy in Finland.

Finnish foreign trade (1968)
     Imports   = $1,593,000,000
     Exports   = $1,636,000,000

NEW ZEALAND:

The main islands are 1,200 miles east of Australia in the South Pacific. The area equals 103,736 square miles. The population in 1968 was 2,776,266. The country is made up of islands:

North Island	44,281 square miles
South Island	59,093 square miles
Stewart Island	670 square miles
Chatham Island	372 square miles

Cook Strait separates North and South Islands. The narrowest width of Cook Strait is sixteen miles. Annually about 100,000 tourists visit New Zealand which has mountains, volcanoes, golden beaches, hot geysers, and spectacular caves. There are fifteen mountains over 10,000 feet high. The highest is Mount Cook.

New Zealand was a British colony which became a dominion in 1907 and independent in 1947. The government includes a Governor General who represents the British Crown. The government has a House of Representatives elected for three years. The Prime Minister and Cabinet are chosen from the House. New Zealand belongs to the United Nations. The native Maoris are Polynesians but there were only 219,042 in 1968. The other New Zealanders are Europeans, mainly British.

New Zealand is mainly agricultural. Wool, meat, and dairy products account for 78% of New Zealand's exports. 13.5% of the population work in agriculture. Food processing is the largest industry. There is a flourishing pulp and paper industry. New Zealand has an iron and steel industry and recently natural gas was discovered on North Island. Education is free and compulsory from ages 7-15 years.

58. Classification and Contrast (Biology)

The following information is about vertebrates and classes of vertebrates.

Listen to the following data:

Vertebrates:
1. have backbones
2. enlarged end of nerve cord (brain) is protected by cartilage or bone
3. most species have appendages in pairs
4. about 45,000 species

Class of vertebrate: reptile
1. young and adults breathe by lungs
2. eggs with shells
3. two pairs of appendages with claws (small or lacking in some species)
4. scales
5. three-chambered heart
6. about 7,000 species

Class of vertebrate: amphibian
    1. young, usually aquatic, with gills
    2. adults terrestrial with lungs
    3. two pairs of appendages (small or lacking in some species)
    4. no claws
    5. three-chambered heart
    6. about 2,800 species
    7. eggs never have shells

Class of vertebrate: bird
    1. feathers (modification of scales)
    2. eggs — shell always hard
    3. front appendages usually modified as wings
    4. four-chambered heart
    5. about 8,600 species

Class of vertebrate: mammal
    1. hairs (modification of scales)
    2. mammary glands of females secrete milk
    3. fewer bones than reptiles
    4. teeth of four types
    5. four-chambered heart
    6. approximately 5,000 species

Class of vertebrate: fish
    1. breathe through gills
    2. two-chambered heart
    3. scales
    4. eggs without shells
    5. appendages as fins

Write a summary of each of the five classes, using complete sentences. Include in your description of each such contrastive data as are necessary so that the reader will really know the differences between the classes.

59. Writing Statements: Review Exercise

Write sentences using the following patterns. RECALL CONTENT from earlier exercises to complete the sentences. You may complete the blanks with as many words as you think necessary.

1. _____ is an outstanding example of _____.
2. Although _____ and _____ are superficially similar, they are different because _____.
3. _____ is an instance of _____.
4. Generally speaking, _____ can be divided into _____ in accordance with _____.
5. That _____ are _____ is a widely held opinion; in my view, however, this statement requires qualification.

6. _____ took place in _____ ; almost simultaneously _____ .
7. _____ and _____ are absolutely dissimilar in _____ .
8. All that most people know about _____ is that _____ ; in my opinion, this is an oversimplification.
9. The _____ of the average _____ ranges from _____ to _____ .
10. The more we learn about _____ , the more _____ .

Introducing Cause and Effect

Read silently while your teacher reads aloud.

Throughout this book you learn a number of basic METHODS of LOGICAL ORGANIZATION. One of these is CAUSE and EFFECT relationships. Cause and effect relationships are often related to CHRONOLOGICAL ORDER in that the result usually follows the cause in time. You must be alert not to confuse the two relationships. NOT EVERY CHRONOLOGICAL SEQUENCE is CAUSE and EFFECT.

A. Decide if the following pairs of sentences are CAUSE and EFFECT or only CHRONOLOGICAL ORDER.

1. Mary has a vitamin C deficiency. Mary has a skin disease.
2. John cut his finger with a sharp knife. John's finger bled.
3. The Jones family went to the movies last Saturday. The Jones children ate popcorn at the movies.
4. Peter's car ran out of gas. Peter had to walk to the nearest gas station.
5. Peter's girl friend hit him on the head with her handbag. Peter's car ran out of gas on the way to the beach.

B. Consider the pairs of sentences in A. Decide which category they fit:

> Necessarily CAUSE and EFFECT
> Probably CAUSE and EFFECT
> Possibly CAUSE and EFFECT
> Unlikely CAUSE and EFFECT
> Unrelated in terms of CAUSE and EFFECT.

C. Join each of the pairs of sentences to form one sentence which clearly indicates the relationship between the two parts.

Structure Vocabulary

so	hence
thus	because
consequently	because of
therefore	owing to
accordingly	since
for this reason	due to
as a result	

_____ is due to _____
_____ is the result of ____
_____ results in _____
_____ is the effect of _____
have an effect on
the reason for _____
the reason is that ____
_____ causes ____
_____ is the cause of ____
_____ follows from _____
If _____ , then _____ follows

If _____ is true, then _____ follows
_____ ; consequently _____
_____ ; therefore _____
the consequence of ____ is ____
as a consequence
so _____ that
such a _____ that
one effect of ____ is that _____
_____ make(s) ____ possible by _____
reversible
irreversible

Composition Exercises

60. Writing Statements of Cause and Effect

Use the structure vocabulary of CAUSE and EFFECT to write statements about the following topics. Each of the topics has appeared in a previous exercise.

Practice the structure vocabulary which is new to you.

1. tourism in Arizona
2. mail delivery
3. education
4. automation
5. paper industry
6. irrigation
7. taxation of Colonial America
8. production and consumption
9. vegetation
10. mobility

61. Cause and Effect (Biology)

In an earlier exercise you were given data about the cooling power of trees and air conditioners. Try to RECALL the CONTENT of the earlier exercises referred to here. If you cannot RECALL the necessary CONTENT VOCABULARY, refer back to the data you need.

A. Write three statements of CAUSE and EFFECT which are TRUE about the data.

B. Write three questions of CAUSE and EFFECT about the data.

C. Write a paragraph in which you explain why people should plant trees near houses.

62. Cause and Effect (Geography)

You have been given data about the mountainous regions of Mexico and Iceland. Try to RECALL the CONTENT of the earlier exercises referred to here. If you cannot RECALL the CONTENT and the necessary CONTENT VOCABULARY, refer back to the data you need. Write a composition in which you explain the CAUSE and EFFECT relationships existing among the elevation, the vegetation, and the population distribution of the two regions.

63. Cause and Effect (Transportation)

A. You have been given data about the Model T Ford, about its production, and about its cost. Write a paragraph in which you explain the CAUSE and EFFECT relationships existing between the rate of production and the retail price of the Model T Ford.

B. Write a composition in which you explain the CAUSE and EFFECT relationships which exist within ONE of the following pairs.

U.S. mobility and the automobile

or

Highway construction and the growth of cities

64. Cause and Effect (Explorers)

In earlier exercises you were given data about exploration and settlement of the United States. You also compared and contrasted 19th century and later explorations.

A. Write five statements of CAUSE and EFFECT based on this information.

B. Write a paragraph about the CAUSE and EFFECT relationships which exist between methods of transportation and ease and speed of exploration.

C. Write a composition in which you discuss the different CAUSE and EFFECT relationships that exist in

(a)   exploration for knowledge, and
(b)   exploration for colonization or settlement.

65. Cause and Effect (Labor)

Listen to the following information.

In 1970 about sixty small and medium-sized factories in the United States adopted a four-day work week. According to the plan, workers work forty hours but instead of the usual five-day week, they now work only four days. Workers are enthusiastic about the three-day weekly vacation. According to management, productivity has increased about 18% since the inception of the new plan. Absenteeism has dropped by 69% and lateness is almost non-existent.

A. Write three statements of CAUSE and EFFECT which are TRUE according to this data.

B. Write three INFERENCES of CAUSE and EFFECT based on this data.

C. Evaluate the INFERENCES you made according to this scale:

NECESSARILY CAUSE and EFFECT
PROBABLY CAUSE and EFFECT
POSSIBLY CAUSE and EFFECT

66. Cause and Effect (Education/Government)

Consider the following information which is out of order.

1. The U.S. constitution makes no provisions about education.
2. The states delegate much of the financial responsibility for education to the towns and cities.
3. The federal government gives some financial aid to the states for education.
4. Schools are run by school boards.
5. Education is the responsibility of the separate states of the U.S.
6. Each state has its own school system.

Write a paragraph of CAUSE and EFFECT about United States education, based on the data.

67. Cause and Effect (Pollution/Weather)

A. Examine the information you are given. Write two statements of COMPARISON or CONTRAST which are TRUE according to the data.

B. Examine the information you are given. Write two statements of CAUSE and EFFECT which are TRUE according to the data.

C. Write two statements of CAUSE and EFFECT which are FALSE according to the data.

D. (a)   On the basis of the evidence cited for Chicago and La Porte, make a statement of GENERAL INFERENCE about EFFECTS of air pollution in GENERAL.
   (b)   Is your statement wholly true, wholly false, or only partially true because of insufficient evidence?
   (c)   To acquire sufficient evidence for your GENERAL INFERENCE to be true, what questions would you need to ask? Write five FACTUAL QUESTIONS whose answers might support your inference.

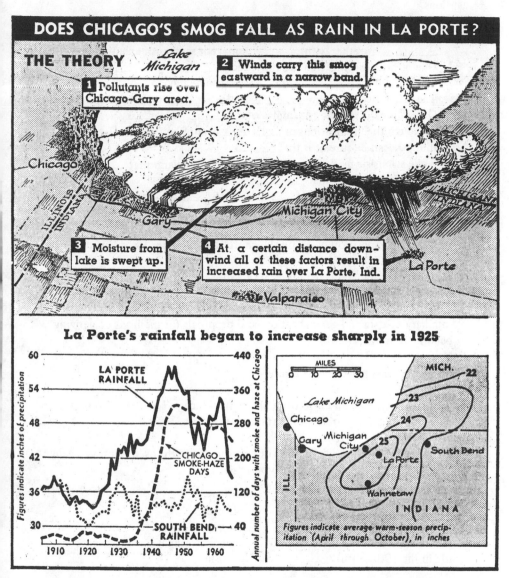

DOES CHICAGO'S SMOG FALL AS RAIN IN LA PORTE?

A striking example of inadvertent climate change is the increased precipitation since 1925 near La Porte, Ind., downwind from Chicago and the steel mills of Gary, Ind. At this distance the mixture of smog and moisture is apparently suitable for producing rain. The precipitation keeps pace with the annual number of hazy days in the Chicago-Gary area, as shown on the chart at left. South Bend, further downwind and not on the centerline of the Chicago smoke cloud, seems largely immune to this influence (dotted line on chart). The map at right shows the region's rainfall pattern.

E. Write sentences of the following patterns, using data from the charts and captions.

1. If it is true that _____ , then _____ .
2. _____ together with _____ make it seem probable that _____ .
3. One of the problems that has intrigued _____ is _____ .
4. If one observes _____ , _____ can be recognized.
5. The difference between _____ and _____ is that _____ .
6. One of the outstanding examples of _____ is _____ .
7. Although the implications of _____ cannot be fully resolved, one thing we can be sure of is that _____ .
8. While scientists may hesitate to make a definite claim that _____ , it must be admitted that _____ .
9. The fundamental causes of _____ are _____ .
10. _____ and _____ are essentially unrelated.

F. Write a short composition based on the charts and captions, using this organization:
   summary of data, and generalization of cause and effect relationship

   or

   summary of data and generalization, and proposals for methods of deriving benefit from this situation.

68. Writing Statements: Review Exercise

The sentence patterns you used to write about the Chicago/LaPorte exercise are generally applicable. They are appropriate for a variety of topics.

A. Write sentences about the following topics using the patterns. (You may change the order of the sentence patterns if you wish.)

prices	biology
education	climate
U.S. government	geography
immunization	manufacturing
life in the 19th century	tourism

B. Choose five of the sentence patterns which you think would make good opening statements for paragraphs. Explain why.

69. Cause and Effect (Place Names)

A. Examine the map of U.S. place names and the data about the language origins of the place names.

B. Refer back to the map of early U.S. immigration routes, page 79.

122

C. On the basis of the evidence provided by the two maps, write a short paragraph of INFERENCE in which you give the reasons for these non-English place names in the United States. Your paragraph will be a SYNTHESIS of more than one source of DATA. Your paragraph will combine:

> INFERENCE
> CHRONOLOGICAL ORDER
> CLASSIFICATION
> CAUSE and EFFECT

FRENCH

SAULT STE. MARIE
DETROIT
VINCENNES
ST. LOUIS
NEW ORLEANS

SPANISH

SAN FRANCISCO
LOS ANGELES
SANTA FE
SAN ANTONIO
GASPARILLA

70. Cause and Effect (Place Names)

As the United States was settled, many towns were founded. Some of these towns were named for the places the immigrants came from. Some were given Indian names, or the names of people, both the names of famous people and those of ordinary settlers. Some settlements were given very distinctive names such as Hell, Michigan; Big Bottom, Ohio; and Bad Axe, Michigan. Often these distinctive names were the result of some interesting happening in the early history of the town.

A. Why do you think Salt Lake City was given that name?

B. Tell why you think the following towns were given their names. You may be as inventive as you wish in the reasons you give. You may invent anecdotes about the town's early history, or ascribe to the town geographical features, peculiar characteristics, etc.

Crooked Falls	Poverty Hill
Milk River Town	Old Mission
Dead-Mule Canyon	Crazy Horse
Hen-Roost	Tombstone

Your REASONS are INFERENCES.

71. Inference and Reverse Chronological Order (Food Production)

In REVERSE CHRONOLOGICAL ORDER the data are organized so that the writer starts with what is most recent and proceeds backwards to what is most remote in time.

The following information about food production is presented in random order.

A. Examine the information. Classify the data into 2 kinds: (a) information which can be presented chronologically, and (b) information which is not necessarily chronological.

B. Examine the information and draw conclusions from it. Make inferences.

C. Write a composition about food production and food resources. Your composition will have several paragraphs. One section of your composition must be organized according to REVERSE CHRONOLOGICAL ORDER. The other sections of your composition can be organized according to any METHOD you CHOOSE (comparison, contrast, cause and effect, etc.). You will probably want to include INFERENCES in your composition.

1. One difficulty in increasing world food resources is the elimination of waste.
2. Much food is wasted; the problem of utilizing wasted resources is primarily that of making people accustomed to new foods.
3. Food authorities estimate that two and a half acres of land are needed to provide an adequate diet for one person.
4. About half of the land surface of the earth is not suitable for farming.
5. Less than one-third of the world's population has a daily diet sufficient in calories.
6. The daily calorie consumption in the United States is 3,250.
7. Food is destroyed in storage by rats and insects or by molds.

8. In the temperate region only five million square miles of a total of forty-one million is good for farming.

9. In many countries agricultural methods have changed little over the last thousand years.

10. Land can be improved by use of fertilizers, rotation of crops, and modern machinery.

11. Enough food is destroyed annually by poor storage to feed 200,000,000 people for a year.

12. In the mid-twentieth century approximately 1.4 acres are being cultivated for each person in the world.

13. In 1800 the U.S. farmer worked 375 hours to produce 100 bushels of wheat.

14. In 1870 each farm worker in the U.S. had 1.6 horsepower.

15. In colonial times 85% of the U.S. population was needed on the farms to produce food.

16. In the mid-twentieth century the average U.S. farm worker has sixty-five horsepower of mechanical energy at his disposal.

17. In 1800 the average U.S. farmer could produce food to support only four persons.

18. Farm tools changed little from ancient times to the 1700's.

19. U.S. farmers worked 10 billion fewer man hours annually in the 1960's than they did in 1920.

20. In 1940 the U.S. farmer produced one hundred bushels of wheat in forty-seven hours of work.

21. In the 1970's fewer than 12% of the U.S. population is engaged in farming, but they provide food for the entire population plus a surplus.

22. Machines for threshing, plowing, and reaping were introduced in the first part of the nineteenth century.

23. Steam engines replaced horsepower for many farm machines in the 1870's.

24. In 1960 more than 5,000,000 tractors operated on U.S. farms.

25. Factory production of tractors started in 1903.

26. Tractors do 95% of the cultivating work on present day U.S. farms.

Introducing Explanation

Read silently while your teacher reads aloud.

Throughout this book you are introduced to various methods of logical organization. One term that is frequently used in written assignments is *explain. To explain* means to make something clear and comprehensible. EXPLANATION can involve a number of logical methods of organization. Substantiation of a generalization is a kind of explanation. The elucidation of a method or of a process is a kind of explanation that involves cause and effect and usually chronological and spatial order. Similarly classification, comparison, and contrast can be used for EXPLANATION.

When you are asked to write an explanation, you must first ask yourself *what logical method is appropriate, and choose the appropriate structure vocabulary.*

Composition Exercises

72. Explanation (Mathematics)

A. The square you see below is commonly called a magic square. Examine it and then write a brief explanation of why it is called a *magic* square.

1	17	16	6
14	8	7	11
10	12	13	5
15	3	4	18

Content vocabulary you may want to use:

sum	vertical	across
addition	horizontal	up and down
subtraction	diagonal	result

B. 1. Write two statements about the magic square which are FALSE.
   2. Write two questions about the applicability of the magic square.
   3. Write one statement of INFERENCE about the discoverer of the magic square.

73. Explanation (Proverbs)

A. Every language has proverbial sayings. The following are proverbial sayings in English.

Spare the rod and spoil the child.
The early bird catches the worm.
Woman's place is in the home.
A penny saved is a penny earned.
Man works from sun to sun but woman's work is never done.
One swallow doesn't make a summer.
People who live in glass houses should never throw stones.
Like father, like son.

Discuss the meaning of each of these sayings. Do you have a similar saying in your culture?

127

B. Write a paragraph of **EXPLANATION** for each of these sayings. You may wish to use **EXAMPLES** or **ANECDOTES**, or to make **CONTRASTS**. Assume that the proverb is new to the reader.

Suggested opening sentence:

English speakers have a proverbial saying " _____ ."

C. Choose a proverbial saying from your own culture. Write a paragraph of **EX-PLANATION**. Assume that the reader is not familiar with the proverb.

74. Cause and Effect, Explanation (Superstition)

Many people believe in superstitions. According to the dictionary a superstition is a belief that some action or circumstance not related to an event influences its outcome. In other words superstitious beliefs are **CAUSE** and **EFFECT** beliefs where there is no cause and effect in operation. The following table lists some superstitions held by superstitious English speakers.

ACTION	*SUPPOSED RESULT*
breaking a mirror	bad luck
number 7	good luck
number 13	bad luck
walking under a ladder	bad luck
opening an umbrella in a house	bad luck
spilling salt	bad luck

A. Make a statement of **GENERALIZATION** about superstitions.

B. Write three questions about the origin of superstitions.

C. Write three **INFERENCES** about superstitious people.

D. Choose one superstition. Write a brief paragraph of **EXPLANATION**. Explain why you think such a belief came to be commonly accepted.

E. Write a brief paragraph about generally held superstitions in your culture.

75. Cause and Effect, and Inference (Government/History)

A. Write a short paragraph in which you explain why the President of the U.S. prefers to have the majority of the members of the Senate and of the House belong to the same political party he does.

B. Write a short paragraph in which you explain the importance of taxation in the development of American-British relations prior to 1776.

76. Explanation (Weather)

Examine the following diagram.

A. Write two statements of COMPARISON or CONTRAST which are TRUE according to the diagram.

B. Write two statements of COMPARISON or CONTRAST which are FALSE according to the diagram.

C. Write one question of CAUSE and EFFECT.

D. Assume you are

    (a)   a geographer
    (b)   a meteorologist
    (c)   a farmer
    (d)   a tourist

For each of these occupations write three questions which ask for additional information about the diagram. Your questions must be relevant to your occupation. Write your questions as *indirect speech.*

E. Write a composition in which you EXPLAIN the process pictured in the diagram that follows.

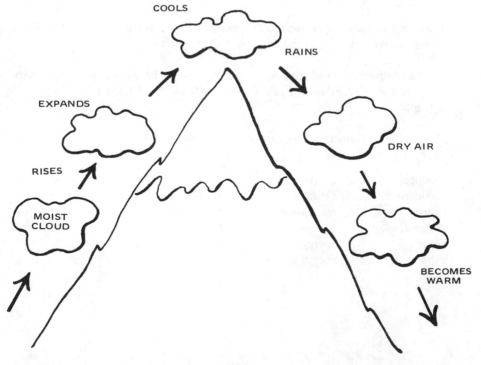

Content vocabulary you may wish to use:

vapor	elevate	atmospheric	drought
vaporize	elevation	precipitation	average
evaporate	moist	stable	vegetation
evaporation	moisture	stability	rain gauge
dense	cool (verb)	instability	crops
density	cool (adj.)	come in contact with	erode
densely	expand	drain	erosion
condense	expansion	drainage	direction
condensation	contract	rain	common
humid	contraction	rainy	uncommon
rise	pressure	dry	phenomenon
fall	atmosphere	arid	phenomena

77. Explanation (Biology)

A. Write three fact questions about the process pictured in the diagram of photosynthesis that follows.

B. Write three statements of CAUSE and EFFECT which are FALSE according to the process pictured in the diagram.

C. Write one statement of CLASSIFICATION for which you have been given IN-SUFFICIENT EVIDENCE.

D. Make a list of factual questions about photosynthesis for which you would like to have answers in order to fully understand the process.

E. Write a composition in which you explain the process involved in photosynthesis. Keep clear the CAUSE and EFFECT relationships and CHRONOLOGICAL sequence.

Content vocabulary you may wish to use:

produce	inhale	absorb	function
production	breathe	absorption	agent
sugar	respiration	chemical reaction	vary
molecule	catalyst	bond	store (verb)
atom	energy	chemical bonding	
exhale	energy source	transfer	

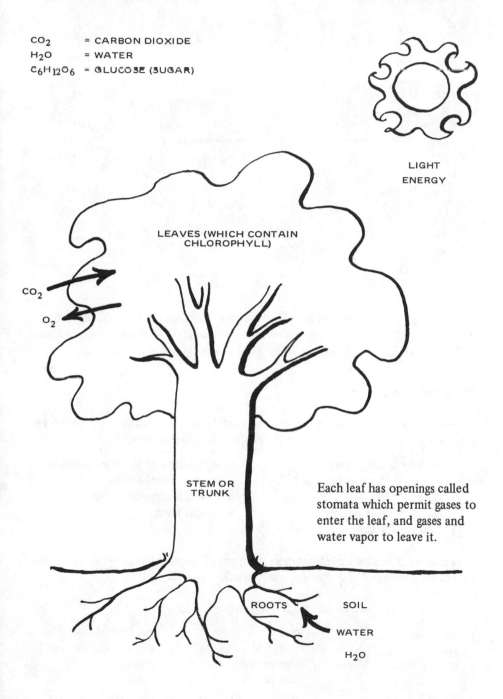

CO_2 = CARBON DIOXIDE
H_2O = WATER
$C_6H_{12}O_6$ = GLUCOSE (SUGAR)

LIGHT ENERGY

LEAVES (WHICH CONTAIN CHLOROPHYLL)

CO_2

O_2

STEM OR TRUNK

Each leaf has openings called stomata which permit gases to enter the leaf, and gases and water vapor to leave it.

ROOTS   SOIL

WATER

H_2O

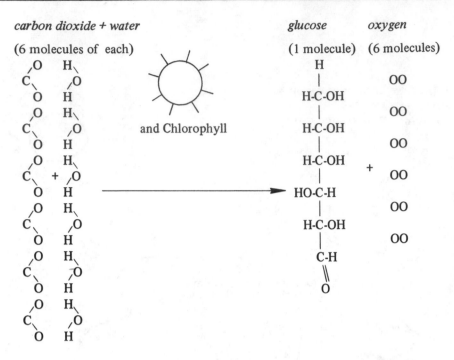

carbon dioxide + water   *glucose*   *oxygen*

(6 molecules of each)   (1 molecule)   (6 molecules)

and Chlorophyll

The energy provided by the sun shining on the chlorophyll in plants allows 6 molecules of CO_2 to combine with 6 molecules of H_2O to produce one molecule of glucose ($C_6H_{12}O_6$). Oxygen (6 molecules) is left over in the process.

78. Explanation (Science)

Choose *one* of the following processes and explain how it operates. You may draw diagrams if you wish but you must also explain the process in words.

1. thunder and lightning
2. eclipse of the sun (or moon)
3. tides
4. action of yeast in bread
5. temperature inversion and smog
6. circulation of blood in humans
7. how a camera works
8. how a thermometer works
9. simple lever

You may want to look up information in an encyclopedia before you write. If you do use an encyclopedia, do *not* copy information; *paraphrase.*

Content vocabulary you may want to use:

discharge	electric	negative charge
cloud	electrical	positive charge
atmosphere	atmospheric	flash
current	sun, solar	moon, lunar
rotate	revolve, revolution	axis, gravity
path	shadow	gravitational pull

orbit	surface	waves, coast
chlorophyll	cell	mold
energy	oxygen	sugar
alcohol	carbon dioxide	beer
bread	expand, expansion	fog
humidity, humid	valley, depression	particles
circulation	artery	vein
capillary	heart	corpuscle
temperature	lungs	mercury
lens	degree	contract, contraction
prism	beam	converge, diverge
focus	image	concave, convex
motion	light waves	effort
machine	weight, heavy	input, output
mechanical advantage	distance	advantage

79. Writing Questions (Science)

Write fact questions about the following topics. Indicate in the appropriate column the kind of answer expected.

TOPIC	QUESTION	KIND OF ANSWER
levers	How many kinds of simple levers are there?	Number Classification
eclipse of the sun		
thermometer		
tides		
smog		
camera		
thunder and lightning		
nutrition		
blood		
photosynthesis		

80. Explanation (Economics)

A. Using the diagram below, explain what happens when Mr. X gives Mr. Y a personal check for $100.

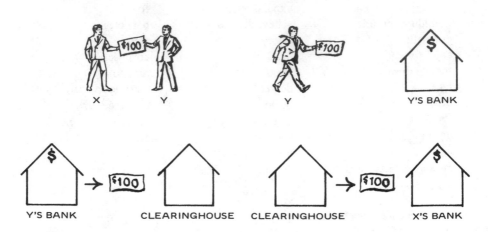

Content vocabulary you may want to use:

exchange	owe	the difference
local	credit	between receipts
member bank	debit	and debits
cash amount	account	deposit
checks drawn upon	credit an account	withdraw
a bank	with	withdrawal
total	settlement	transaction
keep track of		

B. 1. Write three factual questions about the clearinghouse for which you would need answers if you were to accurately describe the function of this institution.
   2. Write three statements of OPINION about the transaction pictured in the diagram for which you have INSUFFICIENT EVIDENCE.
   3. Write three statements which are FALSE according to the diagram.

81. Explanation: Paradox

A paradox is a statement that is seemingly contradictory, but is in fact true. For example, if we say that a rich man's fortune is really worthless, or that a victory was in fact a defeat, we are making statements which are PARADOXICAL.

A. Write a paragraph to explain how the idea of technological *progress* may be considered paradoxical. Use in your paragraph data on air pollution from previous exercises.

B. Psychologists theorize that some people behave aggressively because they are beset by fears. Explain how this is paradoxical.

C. A person is never so lonely as when he is in a crowd. Explain this paradox; substantiate with specific examples.

D. Winning is sometimes losing. Explain; illustrate your explanation with examples.

Introducing Cycles and Chain Reactions

There are two particular kinds of CAUSE and EFFECT of which the student should be aware. The first is known as CHAIN REACTION. In a chain reaction there is a series of events; each part of the series causes its successor. It is common in chemistry and physics but can also be found in non-scientific situations. In a chain reaction

> A causes B
> B causes C
> C causes D, etc.

The other kind of cause and effect relationship is known as a CYCLE. In a cycle there is a series of reactions; each part of the series is linked to its predecessor and its successor. Moreover, the last step in the series is linked to the first step. Cycles are commonly found in zoology, botany and ecology, but they can also be found in non-scientific situations. This is what a cycle looks like.

Composition Exercises

82. Cycle (Biology)

Examine the following information which is not necessarily in the correct sequence. Arrange the data in order to form a paragraph of CAUSE and EFFECT which explains a CYCLE. Add specific examples and illustrations to make your paragraph clear.

Animals get the nitrogen they need by eating plants.

Plants get nitrogen compounds from the soil and join them with carbohydrates to make proteins.

Bacteria turn the waste products of animals into simple nitrogen compounds in the soil.

Nitrogen is returned to the soil in animal wastes.

Like the edge of a wheel, a cycle has no clear beginning or end. In writing about a cycle the student must CHOOSE what seems to him a logical place to begin.

83. Cause and Effect: Cycle (Biology)

Write a paragraph in which you explain the relationships which the following diagram illustrates. Give specific examples for each stage of the cycle.

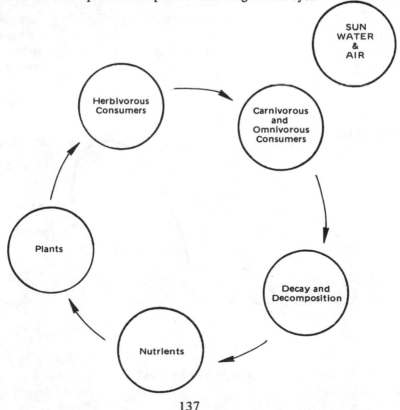

84. Cause and Effect: Cycle (Biology)

A. Write two TRUE statements of COMPARISON and CONTRAST based on the following diagrams of the water cycle.

B. Write two statements of CAUSE and EFFECT which are FALSE according to the diagrams.

C. Write two questions of CAUSE and EFFECT based on the diagrams

D. Write two questions of DEFINITION based on the diagrams.

E. Write one TRUE statement of CLASSIFICATION based on the diagrams.

F. Write an explanation of each of the cause and effect relationships of each of the cycles pictured in the two diagrams.

Content vocabulary you may want to use:

balance	energy	evaporation
unbalanced	drain	consume
imbalance	drainage	consumption
nature	react	decompose
depend on	reaction	decomposition
system	equilibrium	atmosphere
rainwater	salt	atmospheric
precipitation	desalinization	condense
sunshine	breath	condensation
light	evaporate	

SHORT CYCLE

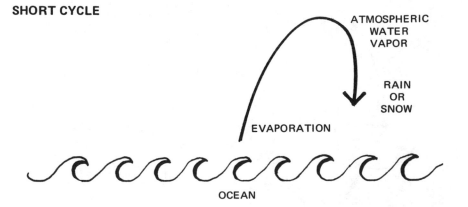

THE WATER CYCLE

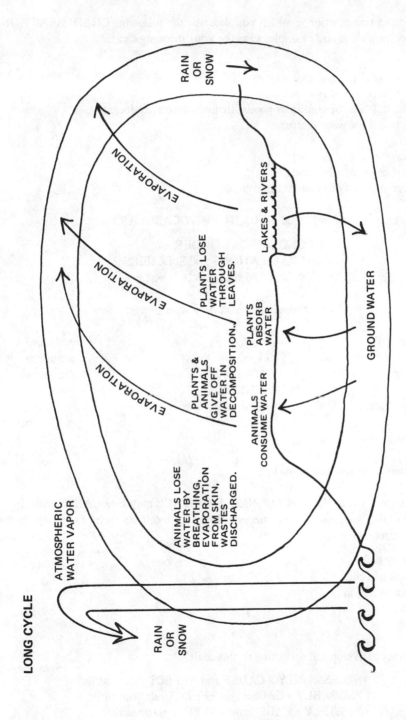

85. Chain Reaction (Economics)

Write a brief composition in which you describe the following CHAIN REACTION. Add specific details and examples to make your meaning clear.

Events:

1. rise in prices of raw materials
2. rise in prices of consumer goods (manufactured products)
3. demand for wage increases
4. strikes
5. wage increases granted
6. higher production costs
7. rise in prices of manufactured goods

For this exercise you will need STRUCTURE VOCABULARY of:

CHRONOLOGICAL ORDER
GENERALIZATIONS and SPECIFICS
CAUSE and EFFECT

Content vocabulary you may wish to use:

go on strike	estimate	produce
strike (noun)	expense	producer
striker	inflation	production
profit	inflationary	goods
expenditures	inflationary spiral	*raise* prices
demand	factory	*rise* in prices

86. Chain Reaction (Nutrition)

We have seen that a CHRONOLOGICAL SEQUENCE may be a CAUSE and EFFECT SEQUENCE but need not necessarily be so. Examine each of the steps in the following sequence:

1. poor soil
2. lack of food
3. malnutrition
4. famine
5. death

Where does each step fall according to this scale?

NECESSARILY a CAUSE and EFFECT relationship
PROBABLY a CAUSE and EFFECT relationship
POSSIBLY a CAUSE and EFFECT relationship
NO CAUSE and EFFECT relationship

A. Write a composition in which you describe a situation where all of the five steps would constitute a CHAIN REACTION, that is, where all five steps are related to each other by CAUSE and EFFECT.

B. Write a composition in which you *alter* the above sequence so that the outcome is different. For example, you may wish to add

importation of food

> *or*

systematic use of fertilizers

> *or*

irrigation

> *or*

manufacture of protein concentrate from fish.

Be sure you explain the relationship between each of your steps.

87. Chronological Sequence and Chain Reaction (Government/Education)

A. Complete each of the following chronological sequences.

1.
2. emigration
3.
4.

1.
2. increase in taxation for schools
3.
4.

1. high rate of illiteracy
2.
3.
4.

1.
2.
3. compulsory education to age 15
4.

B. Examine each of the steps in your sequences. Decide if the step is

> NECESSARILY a CAUSE and EFFECT relationship
> PROBABLY a CAUSE and EFFECT relationship
> POSSIBLY a CAUSE and EFFECT relationship
> NOT a CAUSE and EFFECT relationship

C. For each of your sequences write a composition in which you describe a situation where all of your steps would take place. Explain the relationships between each of your steps in your composition.

88. Explanation and Cause and Effect (Air Pollution)

A. Why does warm polluted air tend to concentrate in the center of large cities? Refer to the following data in order to write a composition of EXPLANATION in answer to this question. You may add information of your own if you like. It may help to draw a diagram in addition to your composition.

1. Warm air rises.
2. The city absorbs heat during the day.
3. Vertical surfaces of buildings collect heat.
4. Warm air expands when it rises.
5. Vertical surfaces of buildings reflect heat.
6. The city absorbs more heat during the day than the open countryside.
7. The city air is polluted.
8. Large, tall buildings are found in the center of large cities.
9. The city retains more heat at night than the open countryside.
10. Cool air from the edge of the city flows into the center.
11. City air contains large amounts of aerosols, tiny particles small enough to remain suspended in the air.
12. A ceiling of pollution can prevent the sun's rays from heating surface air efficiently.
13. Particles in the air move with the circulatory system.
14. Strong winds can alter the self-contained circulation of the air in cities.
15. The circulation of particles in the air forms a ceiling called *dust dome*.

B. Since warm polluted air tends to concentrate in the center of large cities, what advice would you give a government that plans to build an entirely new capital city? Consider city location, in terms of topography and climate, transportation, height of buildings, inclusion of industry.

The information in this exercise is based on "The Special Characteristics of City Weather," *Pollution Primer*, National Tuberculosis and Respiratory Disease Assoc., 1969. Reproduced by permission.

89. Cause and Effect (Economics)

In 1932 in an article called "Why Should Americans Travel to Europe?" U.S. citizens were urged to visit Europe as tourists. Among the reasons given was this CHAIN of CAUSE and EFFECT.

Americans would learn the good qualities of Europeans. This would reduce international tensions. A reduction of international tensions would reduce the danger of war. Ultimately this would lead to a reduction in taxes.

142

A. Assume you can communicate with the author of the article. Write five questions you would ask him concerning his reasoning.

B. Write a paragraph in which you explain to what extent you think the author's claim of cause and effect is reasonable or fallacious.

Content vocabulary:

culture	cold war	eradicate
cultural	diplomacy	moderate
cultural exchange	conflict	influence
necessary relationship	misunderstanding	taxation
necessarily related	alleviate	priority

Introducing Analogy

Read silently while your teacher reads aloud.

Analogies are extended comparisons. Sometimes they are simple in language; sometimes they are highly figurative. An analogy points out the resemblance between things that are of different classes. It points out resemblances in attributes or relations. Some analogies are commonly used and easy to understand, as when we liken life to a journey, or death to darkness. Some analogies are subtle and poetic; others are just ridiculous.

Analogies are useful when they illuminate and clarify meaning. Analogies *do not prove*; they suggest and explain.

A. Consider the following analogies. Write a sentence for each in which you explain whether you think the analogy is good or not.

   1. Society is like a barrel of apples. If one of the apples is rotten, the whole barrelful will be spoiled.
   2. Hunters do not shoot at big animals with small bullets. Do not look for a job without a large knowledge of the words of the English language.

B. A detailed analysis of an analogy often makes the comparison seem ridiculous. Analyze the following analogies to show how they are meaningful only if they are not accepted on a literal point-by-point basis.

   Climbing a mountain is analogous to life.
   The President is like the pilot of a ship.
   Money is like rain.
   Training a wife is like training a wild horse.

C. Politicians and propagandists often use analogies *as proof*. Such use of an analogy is fallacious but it may be very persuasive. Assume you are a writer of political propaganda. Write a paragraph in which you attack your political opponents (attack their persons, their actions, their ideology) by using an analogy.

Composition Exercises

90. Analogy and Explanation (Fine Arts)

> Read silently while your teacher reads aloud.

A. In a lecture in which he was discussing the value of the arts, Boris Goldovsky, a twentieth-century world famous expert in opera, said: "I would rather be Mozart's partner than the president of the whole world."

EXPLAIN what you think he might have meant by *partner* in this context.

B. Write a brief paragraph about any of the arts or sciences in which you use a *partner* ANALOGY. Your meanings need not be the same as Boris Goldovsky's. Be sure your paragraph makes the meaning of your ANALOGY clear.

91. Analogy and Explanation (Economics)

Use the following historical information as an explanatory analogy in a short composition of EXPLANATION of checks and traveler's checks. In your composition you should explain what a check is and how it is used, and in what way traveler's checks differ from personal checks.

> Metal money has the disadvantage of being heavy and easily stolen. Early in the Middle Ages merchants formed the habit of carrying with them on their travels not actual coins but written evidence of their ability to pay in coins. These letters or documents were not themselves money but were certificates from some person or institution of known repute, declaring that the merchant had on deposit coinage of a certain amount and that creditors could get payment out of the sum deposited from the person or institution.

92. Inference, Cause and Effect: Review

Write one statement for each of the following topics. Your sentence must state a CAUSE and EFFECT relationship. RECALL the CONTENT of earlier exercises related to the topics; make INFERENCES of CAUSE and EFFECT about the data in earlier exercises.

TOPIC

1. immunization
2. communication
3. life in the U.S. before 1776

TOPIC

4. education in U.S. pioneer settlements
5. world population
6. inventions

145

93. Comparison and Contrast, and Inference (Sociology/Geography)

Use the following data about nomadic life to write a composition of COMPARISON and CONTRAST about nomadic life and urban life. Because you are given insufficient data about nomadic life, you will have to draw INFERENCES about the life of nomads, from the data. Use your own experience to provide GENERALIZATIONS about urban life. Consider the following general aspects:

> education
> mobility
> source of wealth
> family life
> use of natural resources

You may add other general categories if you wish.

Grazing animals soon deplete the desert grass and shrubs.
The most famous of all nomads are the Bedouins who live in the Arabian Desert.
Nomads must keep moving on to fresh pastures.
Nomads live in tents that can be easily moved.
Nomadic culture is passed on by oral tradition.
The largest Bedouin tribe had about 3,000 tents and 75,000 camels in the 1960's.
The herdsmen scatter to find grass for their animals.
Sheep, camels, goats, and horses are owned by Bedouins whose wealth is assessed by the number of animals they own.
Most nomads are illiterate.
Camel dung is used for fuel.
The nomads trade for some food (like coffee, sugar, salt), cloth, and weapons; they sell all the animals they can spare.
Goats and camels provide milk which forms a basic part of the nomad's diet.
Tents are made from black goat-hair cloth.
Sandals are made from camel hide.

94. Classification (Weather/Geography)

Utilize the following data to write a theme of CLASSIFICATION. You may not wish to use all the data given; use only what is RELEVANT to your *method* of classification.

Your first sentence should be a general statement of classification.

Enumerate examples for each of your categories.

Winds

Designation	Miles per hour (Velocity)
calm	less than 1
light breeze	4-7
strong breeze	25-31
gale	39-46
storm	55-63
violent storm	64-73
hurricane	74+

Tornadoes arise when the conditions that cause thunderstorms are unusually violent. They are usually recognized by their funnel shape and loud roar. Winds may blow more than 300 mph around the edges of the tornado. The cone acts like a power vacuum upon everything it passes. Roofs are torn from houses, windows explode outwards, etc. The path is usually around 50 yards wide. The storm moves at 25-40 mph.

Hurricanes are severe cyclones originating over tropical waters. Winds are over 73 mph. The area of strong winds takes the form of a circle or oval (sometimes 500 miles in diameter). Hurricanes move 10-15 mph. Hurricanes start at sea and usually move across open water. They often also sweep over islands, peninsulas, and coasts. They cause damage. Waves from the hurricane also often cause floods. Hurricanes are given the names of girls.

Blizzards are characterized by low temperatures and strong winds bringing large amounts of snow. Winds are 35 mph +. The snow reduces visibility to 500 feet or less.

Number of Tornadoes in U.S., and Deaths

Year	Number	Deaths
1965	915	299
1966	570	105
1967	912	116
1968	660	131

Number of Tornadoes 1916 — 1968: 15,945 with 10,180 deaths

Principal Tornadoes

1965	April 11	Ind., Ill., Mich., Wis.	271 deaths
1966	March 3	Jackson, Miss.	57
1966	March 3	Mississippi, Alabama	61
1966	June 8	Kansas	17
1967	April 21	Illinois	33
1968	May 15	Arkansas	34

Hurricanes, Blizzards, and Deaths

1965	Sept. 7-10 "Betsy"	Fla., Miss., La.	74 deaths
1966	June 4-10 "Alma"	east United States	51 deaths
1966	Sept. 24-30 "Inez"	Fla., Mexico	293 deaths
1966	Blizzard Nov. 4	Midwest, east United States	37 deaths
1967	Sept. 5-25 "Beulah"	Mexico, Texas	54 deaths
1967	Blizzard Dec. 12-20	southwest United States	51 deaths

Speed of Winds in the United States through 1968

	Average mph.	*High mph.*
Boston, Mass.	13.1	65
Chicago, Ill.	10.3	60
Cleveland, Ohio	10.9	74
Detroit, Mich.	10.0	77
Galveston, Texas	11.1	120
Jacksonville, Fla.	8.8	82
Memphis, Tenn.	9.2	56
Miami, Fla.	9.0	80
New Orleans, La.	8.5	98
New York, N.Y.	9.5	70
Philadelphia, Pa.	9.6	73
Salt Lake City, Utah	8.6	71
San Francisco, Calif.	10.4	62
Washington, D.C.	9.4	78

95. Spatial Order (Color/Size)

Mr. and Mrs. Smith want to plant a garden in their backyard along a fence which separates their lot from their neighbor's property. The fence is four feet tall and seven yards long. It runs north-south. The Smith's back door and the windows at the back of the house face due west. There is a tall shade tree in the northern portion of the neighbor's yard which shades about one-third of the fence area. Mr. and Mrs. Smith want to grow several kinds of plants. Here are the characteristics of the plants they have chosen:

Plant	Color	Height	Spacing Requirements	Sun/Shade Requirements (if relevant)
#1	3 varieties: lavender, blue, or pink	12"	Will spread to 12"-15" clumps.	grow best with afternoon sun
#2	3 varieties: scarlet, pink, or white flowers	4 ft. or more	These are climbing roses which will climb along fences. Plant at least 8-9 feet apart.	
#3	pink and white flowers	40"	Plant 1-2 feet apart to provide good circulation of air. Plants will spread. Subject to fungus.	
#4	colors range from pale yellow to orange	3-4 ft.	These lilies have many blooms on each plant. Will spread. Plant at least 1 ft. apart.	filtered light
#5	3 varieties: yellow, orange, or red	24"	Flowers are 6" in diameter	need full sun
#6	yellow, or yellow with red centers	30"	Plant 9-12" apart	need full sun
#7	2 varieties: violet, or white	6"	Plant 1 ft. apart. Will spread	for white variety semi-shade; for violet either sun or shade

Write a composition in which you recommend to the Smiths where they should plant each kind of flower. Keep in mind the plants' need for shade or space; also the colors. Keep in mind the relative heights of each plant. You may make the flower bed as wide as you wish so that you can place small plants in front of big ones. If you wish, you may draw a diagram to accompany your composition. Make the written instructions specific as to relative position and the number of each kind of plant the Smiths should buy.

96. Classification and Spatial Order (Music/Fine Arts)

Examine the following data about the modern symphony orchestra. Write a short composition of CLASSIFICATION in which you:

A. Group the instruments according to type:

1. strings
2. woodwinds
3. brasses   (four major classes of instruments)
4. percussion

B. Consider the relative size of each major section and/or instrument.

C. Describe the relative positions of each orchestral section on the stage. Combine all three kinds of information (from A, B, and C) in your composition. Your composition will be a *summary* of CLASSIFICATION and description.

The modern symphony orchestra has from 60 to 100 musicians. The average orchestra has 96 players. Typical composition of a modern symphony orchestra includes:

xylophone	1 piccolo (sometimes)
12 violas	1 harp
3 flutes	10 cellos
4 horns	kettle drums
18 first violins	3 bassoons
3 oboes	1 double bassoon (sometimes)
3 clarinets	10 double basses
3 trumpets	3 trombones
16 second violins	bass drum
1 bass clarinet (sometimes)	1 tuba
1 English horn	cymbals, tambourine, triangle, rattles

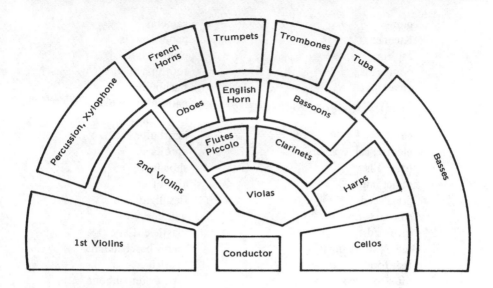

97. Classification and Spatial Order (Business)

The following list represents the kinds of items for sale in Mr. Smith's general store.

A. Group them according to category.

B. Write a *general statement* of *classification* about the merchandise Mr. Smith sells.

C. Choose ONE CATEGORY in which you think Mr. Smith is *understocked.* Write a brief recommendation telling him

(a)   what other merchandise in this category he should stock
(b)   and why.

D. Write one statement of INFERENCE about Mr. Smith's business based on the merchandise list.

E. Write a report for Mr. Smith in which you advise him about how he should arrange the merchandise in his store. Assume that his store has only one floor, is rectangular in shape, has windows in front only and has one front entrance. Your report should include specific instructions about each category of merchandise he sells. You may recommend that he buy additional items if you wish.

Mr. Smith's General Store Merchandise List

lawn mowers	tennis socks
irons	shaving lotion
electric knives	baseball hats for boys
soap	bottle openers
paper plates	birthday cards

gum
Kleenex
aspirin
combs
envelopes
detergents
razor blades
candy
electric can openers
baseballs
paper cups
grass seed
suntan lotion
birdseed
men's sport shirts
fish food
pipe tobacco
handkerchiefs
fishing tackle

cameras
paper towels
electric fans
tooth paste
flashbulbs
paperback books
dog collars
lightbulbs
aprons
shoe laces
cigarettes
flashlights
hair curlers
plastic cutlery
men's baseball hats
lipstick
typewriter ribbons
swim trunks

98. Spatial Order (Fine Arts/Drama)

Mr. Jones is an artist who is interested in the theatre. He has a friend who is a playwright who has asked him to make suggestions for the set for a new play he is writing.

Here is a diagram of the stage on which the play will be performed.

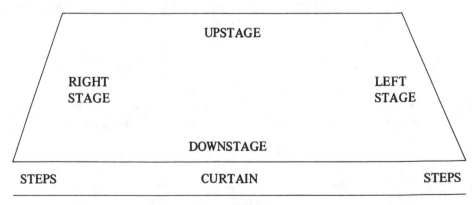

The following is a summary of the information Mr. Jones has about the play.

The action takes place in the livingroom of a very poor, rural family. The set should emphasize their poverty. The mood is one of quiet despair. The playwright wants the set to include a large window looking out on fields and a barn. There must be places for four actors to sit. The date of the setting of the play is the early 1900's. The action takes place somewhere in the Midwest.

A. Write a preliminary outline, describing what the set should look like. Include specific details on furniture and props, including color and relative size. Remember that this is a tentative outline; your advice should be written as suggestions rather than definite instructions.

B. (1)   Write five questions about rural life in the United States in the 1900's that would help you better design the set.
   (2)   Write five questions about the cast and costuming that would help you better design the set.
   (3)   Write three statements about the relationship between the costuming and the furnishing of the set that you consider essential.

Introducing Prediction

Read silently while your teacher reads aloud.

Throughout these exercises you have been asked to make INFERENCES. PREDIC-TION is a special kind of inference in which we foretell (i.e., tell in advance) what we think will happen in the future. Obviously, no one can foresee the future accurately, but logical predictions are far from impossible. If you examine available data, you can often conclude logically what is likely to happen next. In writing PREDIC-TION, you must check carefully your verb tenses. You must distinguish between your statement of prediction which you are making *now* and the events you are predicting which will happen in the *future*.

Structure Vocabulary
(to be used in addition to CAUSE and EFFECT vocabulary)

predict (that)	most likely consequences
make a prediction about	inevitable outcome
infer (that)	the next step
future (adj.)	probability of
in the future	the end result
probable result(s)	likely (adj.)
predictable	the future implications of _____
projected	the future will bring _____
projection	plan (noun)
próject (noun) projéct (verb)	plan to
It is likely (predictable, etc.) that	presume
foresee	presumption
foretell	foreseeable
forecast	in the foreseeable future

Composition Exercises

99. Prediction (Air Pollution/Economics)

A. Turn to the air pollution data about Chicago and the rainfall in the neighboring cities.

Write three statements of PREDICTION based on the data.

B. Turn to the exercise in which you were given comparative prices of food.

Write three statements of PREDICTION based on the data.

100. Prediction (Labor)

Consider the following data which are presented in *random* order.

1. In ancient Greece and Rome much of the labor was performed by slaves.
2. The British government passed legislation approving the right of workers to join labor unions in 1825.
3. Early unions were craft unions.
4. In the 1960's about 18 million Americans belonged to unions.
5. In Europe in the Middle Ages agricultural workers were "bound" to the soil; apprentices and workers under the guild system were paid largely in food, shelter, and clothing.
6. During the Industrial Revolution the labor movement received great impetus, particularly in England.
7. In the early nineteenth century, children as young as five and six years old, worked twelve, fourteen, or even sixteen hours a day in factories, mills, and mines.
8. Child labor laws were passed to regulate the working conditions of children.
9. In 1938 the U.S. Congress passed the Fair Labor Standards Act. The act set child labor standards and fixed minimum wage standards.
10. In the nineteenth and early twentieth centuries many workers worked up to fifteen hours daily
11. In the 1960's the average work week was forty hours.
12. In 1970 several factories in the United States adopted a forty-hour four-day work week.

A. Write a paragraph about the ratio of work and leisure of workers. Organize your data in REVERSE CHRONOLOGICAL ORDER. Some of your information is IMPLICIT rather than EXPLICIT in the given data.

B. Write two statements of PREDICTION based on the data about child labor.

C. Write a paragraph of PREDICTION about the number of hours people will work in the future.

101. Prediction (Population Effects)

Examine the world population charts you used earlier in this book.

A. On the basis of the charts, write three statements of PREDICTION about world population in the future.

B. On the basis of the charts, write a composition of PREDICTION about one of the following:

> the world food supply in the future
> the world fuel supply in the future
> space travel in the future
> family life in the future

102. Generalization and Synthesis (Population)

A. Examine the world population charts.

B. Look again at the statistics on U.S. population growth until 1920. Using both sources, write a statement of GENERALIZATION about the rate of population growth of the United States. (You can assume that the percentage rate of growth for North America = U.S.)

C. Make a generalization about U.S. population growth every hundred years.

D. Use your generalization from C. as your opening sentence for a brief paragraph.

E. Using both sources, could you predict the population of the United States in 3000? Write a sentence of PREDICTION.

F. Use your prediction from E. as the opening sentence for a paragraph. Be sure to include specific information from both sources.

103. Prediction (Autobiography)

Write a composition of PREDICTION in which you tell what you think your own life will be like in the future. Be sure to make clear on what facts you base your predictions about yourself.

104. Prediction (Technology/Labor)

Listen to the following information.

The first electric calculator started operation in 1946. In the early 1950's computers were first produced in quantity. Production of computers using transistors started in the early 1960's. Development of computers has been so rapid that they become obsolete quickly.

Computers are put to many diverse uses in the United States. They are used for air traffic control, long distance phone calls, hotel reservations, payroll computation, billing, and accounting, to name only a few uses. They are widely used not only in business but also in science, engineering, and research.

A. Write a composition in which you PREDICT how computers will be used in the future and the EFFECT the use of computers will have on society.

B. Do you think machines will replace human labor in the future? Write a composition in which you PREDICT how man will regard the concept of *work* in the future. You may wish to CLASSIFY work in your composition. You may wish to CONTRAST with work in the past. Be sure you give REASONS for your PREDICTIONS.

105. Prediction (Education)

Listen to the following information.

The invention of the printing press in the fifteenth century revolutionized education. However, not all the changes brought about by the availability of books came immediately. Many people think a similar revolution in education may be brought about by audio-visual media. Schools now use films, record players, tape recorders, and television in their instructional programs.

Write a composition in which you PREDICT the changes which audio-visual media will bring about in education in the next one hundred years. Your composition should include a CLASSIFICATION of the kinds of changes. It should explain the CAUSE and EFFECT relationships involved. You may also COMPARE and CONTRAST your predicted changes with educational changes in the past.

106. Prediction in Past Time

Usually we make predictions *now* (present time) about the *future* (future time).

It is possible to talk and write about predictions which were made in the past. For example, we can talk about a prediction which a famous man made in the past about his own future.

> *DIRECT SPEECH:*
> Lincoln said, "I predict that the United States will survive the Civil War and remain one united country."

INDIRECT SPEECH:

>   Lincoln predicted that the United States would survive the Civil War as one united country.

or

>   I think Lincoln probably predicted that the United States would survive the Civil War . . .

Often we do not know the actual words of prediction which were spoken in the past. Frequently we can INFER what the prediction might have been.

Using indirect speech, write a statement of prediction in the past for each of the following persons. Your statement will be a kind of INFERENCE. Your statement will tell what you think _____ might have predicted in _____

person   year

about _____ .

topic

1. Lincoln	Homestead Act	1862
2. George III	taxation	1770
3. ordinary U.S. citizen	Pony Express	1860
4. Pilgrims	their new colony	1620
5. Pasteur	immunization	1885
6. doctor	Kennedy's health	1954
7. Lindbergh	air travel	1926
8. meteorologists	weather in Chicago	1920
9. Marconi	communication	1894
10. university officials	revenues from sports	1966

You have information about each topic in earlier exercises. Find the appropriate exercise before you write. Be sure to check the dates for each. RECALL appropriate vocabulary before you write. You do not want to have the same kind of sentence for each of your answers. Try a variety of ways of expressing PREDICTION.

107. Cause and Effect, and Inference (Air Pollution)

A. Write a brief summary in which you COMPARE and CONTRAST the *factual evidence* you are given in the following graphs.

B. What INFERENCE is it possible to make from these data?

1. Write a very general statement of INFERENCE based on the information.
2. Write a QUALIFIED statement of INFERENCE based on the information.
3. Write four questions you would want to ask the researchers who compiled these data before drawing any positive cause and effect conclusion from the data.
4. Write a statement of CAUSE and EFFECT which these data do not prove.
5. Write a statement of PREDICTION based on these data.

158

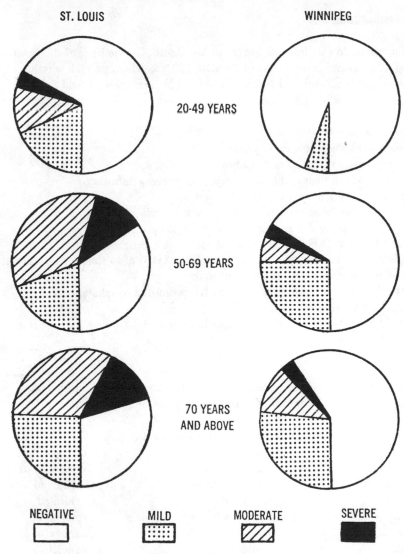

ST. LOUIS   WINNIPEG

20-49 YEARS

50-69 YEARS

70 YEARS
AND ABOVE

NEGATIVE   MILD   MODERATE   SEVERE

Prevalence of Emphysema in Two Cities
With Contrasting Levels of Air Pollution

Prevalence of emphysema, as found in a 1960-66 post mortem examination of the lungs of 300 residents of heavily industrialized St. Louis, Missouri and an equal number from relatively unpolluted Winnipeg, Canada. The subjects were well matched by sex, occupation, socio-economic status, length of residence, smoking habits, and age at death. The findings clearly suggest a link between air pollution and pulmonary emphysema

From: *Pollution Primer*, National Tuberculosis and Respiratory Disease Assoc., 1969.
Reproduced by permission.

108. Prediction (Business)

A. Examine the following information about Mr. Smith. On the basis of this information write a brief composition of PREDICTION in which you tell whether or not you think Mr. Smith will succeed in life as a businessman. Should the bank give him a loan? Why or why not?

1. born on a farm in Arizona
2. mother died when he was six years old
3. delivered papers after school as a boy
4. worked while in high school as a grocery clerk every Saturday
5. bought his first car for $300 at eighteen
6. used his car to deliver groceries for the local grocery store
7. served in the army as a private for two years; no promotions
8. arrested once (age nineteen) for speeding; no other criminal record
9. applied at age twenty-two to bank for loan of $10,000 to start a shoe store in his home town; bank refused him the loan
10. worked as clerk in shoe store for six years; promoted to assistant manager after three years
11. applied at age twenty-eight to bank for loan of $10,000 to start a shoe store in his home town

In your composition it will be necessary to consider aspects of Mr. Smith's life other than those listed. (For example, how much money has he saved?)

Content vocabulary you may wish to use:

success	bad judgment	overambitious
successful	good judgment	(un)trained
succeed	persistent	(un)skilled
fail	persistence	experienced
failure	wise	finances
in error	wisdom	financial
disaster	hardworking	
disastrous	ambitious	

109. Cause and Effect, and Prediction (Nutrition/Education)

Listen to the following data which are presented in *random* order.

1. Malnutrition retards physical growth.
2. Children reared in poverty tend, on the average, to do poorly on tests of intelligence.
3. It is not easy to assess the results of dietary deficiencies in man.
4. In humans the infant brain attains 80% of adult weight by the age of three.
5. In rats and pigs the brain reaches 80% of the adult size by weaning time.

6. During the period of rapid growth the brain is vulnerable to damage due to malnutrition.
7. Animal experiments suggest that good nutrition during the first three years of human life is crucial.
8. At age three the average body weight of humans is 20% of mature body weight.
9. Lack of protein is a serious problem.
10. In baby rats and baby pigs lack of protein causes behavioral changes and reduces the animals' capacity to learn at a later stage.
11. Experiments with rats and pigs suggest that protein intake is related to brain function.
12. Rats born of malnourished mothers are deficient in their capacity to learn.

A. Write a composition of CAUSE and EFFECT in which you explain the relationship which seems to exist between nutrition and learning.

B. Write a composition of PREDICTION in which you tell the actions you think governments will take with respect to education when they are convinced of the validity of the relationship between protein intake and learning ability in the young.

The data in this exercise are based on:

"Nutrition and Learning," Eichenward, H.F. and Fry, P.C., *Science*, Vol. 163, pp. 644-648, 14 February 1969.
"Malnutrition, Learning, and Behavior," Abelson, P.H., *Science*, Vol. 164, p. 17, 4 April 1969.

110. Writing Questions: Review Exercise

Write a question for each of the following topics. Your question must require the kind of answer designated. Review vocabulary before you write.

TOPIC	QUESTION	KIND OF ANSWER
communication	How many methods of communication are available to the average U.S. citizen?	Classification
pollution		Cause
U.S. history		Yes/No
population		Place
weather		Method, Process
government		Name of Person
education		Contrast

Level Three Exercises

Instructions

Read silently while your teacher reads aloud.

The exercises in this book increase in difficulty. Obviously, the final section will be more difficult than the earlier sections. In the middle section of the book you are asked to RECALL earlier vocabulary and to combine METHODS of LOGICAL ORGANIZATION. You are also asked to make INFERENCES and ASSOCIA-TIONS. However, in the middle section, you are still provided with much of the data you are to manipulate. Furthermore you are given little choice about *what* you are to say or *how* you are to say it. In other words, the material in the first two sections is highly CONTROLLED.

In the final section you are allowed to CHOOSE for yourself both content and method more and more. You must make more ASSOCIATIONS and INFER-ENCES than before. You are helped to develop personal CHOICE in personal expression.

Here are the instructions you are to follow for the final series of exercises.

BEFORE YOU WRITE:
A. ASK YOURSELF QUESTIONS ABOUT the CONTENT IDEAS in this exercise. Don't look back at the text unless you have to refresh your memory.
B. RECALL the CONTENT IDEAS and VOCABULARY of earlier exercises that are related to this SUBJECT. Look back at these exercises if you need to refresh your memory.
C. ASK YOURSELF QUESTIONS ABOUT THE METHODS of organization you can use. TRY to remember the STRUCTURE VOCAB-ULARY you can use for each method.
D. Make ASSOCIATIONS, RELATIONSHIPS, and INFERENCES based on other exercises in this book, your own experiences, reading, etc.
ASK YOURSELF QUESTIONS IN ENGLISH.
THINK IN ENGLISH.

Now you are ready to write.

Your composition will combine:

YOUR CHOICE of CONTENT IDEAS from the text,

YOUR CHOICE of METHODS OF ORGANIZATION from the text,

and

YOUR OWN ASSOCIATIONS, RELATIONSHIPS, AND INFERENCES.

For most of the composition exercises in this section, you should write:

AT LEAST 30 MINUTES

AT LEAST 250-300 WORDS.

Of course, for some compositions, you may want to write more.

Introducing Definition

Read silently while your teacher reads aloud.

One major method of logical organization is DEFINITION. Basically, DEFINITION is the explanation of the meaning of a word or phrase so that its meaning is perfectly clear and distinguishable from that of other words or phrases. In writing, we use DEFINITION to make absolutely clear to the reader what we are trying to say.

In writing, there are two main kinds of definition: (a) the dictionary or scientific definition and (b) the personal definition. The former can often be formulated in one sentence; the latter may need many sentences.

A one-sentence definition usually:

1. names the term being defined
2. puts the terms in a general class or category
3. tells the distinguishing characteristics which make the term being defined different from others in the same class or category.

	class	distinguishing feature(s)

_____ is a kind of _____ which _____
             form
             species
             category
             device, etc.

A. Write a one-sentence definition for each of the following:

wristwatch	civil war
cafeteria	kindergarten
chain	dictionary
student	overcoat
passport	washing machine

Note: In writing your definition, you must make sure that the CLASS is clear. For example, it is not very helpful to say a watch is a *thing*.

167

Also, in writing your definition, you must make sure that you distinguish between the other members of the CLASS. For example, your definition of wristwatch should make clear that a wristwatch is not

> the sun
> an alarm clock
> a sundial
> the stars.

All of these are also used to tell the time.

Similarly, if you are to explain clearly what a cafeteria is, you must make sure that your definition clearly distinguishes it from a restaurant, a kitchen in a home, and so on.

B. Which of the words in A was the hardest to define in one sentence? Why? What generalization about one-sentence definitions can you make based on the problems you had defining this word?

C. When we are defining something concrete we can usually use the form:

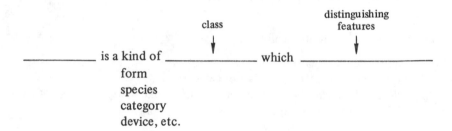

When we are defining abstract concepts, we need to use terms like:

aspect	property
characteristic	condition
method	

What pronoun should you use to substitute for these words?

D. Which of the following are abstract? Which are concrete?

beauty	desk	cup
discipline	truth	justice
flower	escalator	refrigerator
law	dream	ice cream

Discuss your answers. Are there any words in the list that are difficult to decide about? Why?

Try to formulate a one-sentence definition for each of these words. Do not use a dictionary. Which words are hard to define? Why?

When we define abstract concepts, we frequently cannot use a one-sentence formula. We need to explain what the words mean to us. A word like *truth*, for example, means different things to different people. For such words we need to write a PERSONAL DEFINITION.

Structure Vocabulary

to define	to explain
in definition	in explanation
in other words	by _____ is meant
to clarify	to paraphrase
in clarification	

Words like:		
	form	aspect
	species	characteristic
	class	method
	device	property
	type	condition
	kind	attribute
	category	

Composition Exercises

111. Definition by Giving a Synonym or Antonym

> Read silently while your teacher reads aloud.

When we are asked to give the meaning of a word, we usually reply by giving a synonym or by supplying an antonym. For example, if we are asked the meaning of *melancholy*, we may say that it means *sad* or is the opposite of *happy*. This kind of definition is often satisfactory but is not always reliable because synonyms are not always exact substitutes, and antonyms are not always exact opposites. It can frequently lead to circular definitions as when *dishonor* is defined as the opposite of *honor*. We often cannot use this kind of simple definition for complex concepts. For example, to say that *war* is the opposite of *peace* is not a very profound way to define *peace*. Similarly, to say a *Democrat* is the opposite of a *Republican* is misleading.

Why are the following definitions inadequate?

1. Gambling is a way to make money without working.
2. An address is where somebody lives.
3. Socialism is an anti-American philosophy of government.
4. A high school is a place where students study.
5. Neutrality is a state between war and peace.

112. Definition: Using Examples

A. We can look up the meanings of words in a dictionary. Look up the following words in an English-English dictionary:

> home
> family
> beauty

Copy the dictionary definition.

B. Contrast the dictionary definition with what these words mean to you personally. A dictionary definition is often inadequate because we want to express what the word means to *us*. There are two kinds of definitions:

1. DICTIONARY AND SCIENTIFIC
2. PERSONAL

Usually a personal definition requires more than one sentence.

C. Write three separate paragraphs in which you tell what *home, family,* and *beauty* mean to you. To make your meaning absolutely clear to the reader you will probably want to use examples, or to tell an anecdote.

Use one of these suggested sentences to begin your paragraph:

1. By _____ I mean _____ .
2. One of the best ways to illustrate what I mean by _____ is by giving examples.
3. One of the best ways to illustrate what I mean by _____ is by telling the following anecdote.

Content vocabulary you may want to use:

consist of	by marriage	sensory	arts
relatives	homeland	customs	participate
relations	by blood	orphan	please (verb)
related to	by law	adopt	is pleasing to
safety	family	adoption	pleasant, pleasure
dwelling	culture	kith and kin	stimulate
spirit	imagination	close relatives	stimulation
origin	respond	feeling	imagine
native	responsive	sensation	
marry	senses	observe	

113. Definition: Using Examples

A good definition should include more than a list of examples. It is possible, however, to clarify a definition of a complex idea by citing examples or anecdotes.

A. Write examples or anecdotes that could be used in a longer definition of

justice	commerce
patriotism	communication
fine arts	imperialism

B. Write a composition of PERSONAL DEFINITION in which you use examples. You may choose any topic you wish.

114. Definition: Process

Although an adequate definition should include more than a list of examples, it can be improved and clarified by the use of examples, descriptions of procedures, anecdotes, and analogies. All of these can contribute to the effectiveness of a written definition, especially of a complex concept.

A. List three topics for definition that could be made more effective by the inclusion of a description of a process or procedure.

B. Write a paragraph of definition including a description of a process or procedure. Choose one of your topics from A above, or from the following list:

communication	immunization
automation	credit card
football	voting
tennis	legislation
self-service	pollution
photography	agriculture
mining	

115. Definition by Negation

One method of defining a complex concept is to explain what the concept *is not*. This is DEFINITION by NEGATION.

1. Make a list of five concepts and ideas for which you have a PERSONAL DEFINITION. Choose words that mean something special to you.

2. Write a paragraph of definition for two of your words. In order to make clear what you mean, you may want to tell the reader what you *do not mean.* That is, you may want to DEFINE by NEGATION.

   Suggested sentences to begin your paragraph:

   (a) By _____ I do not mean _____ .
   (b) To explain what I mean by _____ , let me first tell you what I do not mean.
   (c) One of the best ways to explain what I mean by _____ is by giving examples of what I do not mean.

116. Definition by Contrast

When we write about complex topics, it is essential that the reader know exactly what the terms we use mean. It is often helpful to use a contrast to make clear exactly what we mean. Note that we are making a personal definition, *not* a dictionary definition.

Using definition and contrast, make clear the distinction between four of the following pairs:

socialism and communism	evolution and change
work and slavery	humor and sarcasm
famine and hunger	a house and a home
malnutrition and hunger	work and drudgery
literacy and education	cruelty and discipline
freedom and discipline	a friend and an acquaintance

172

Suggested opening sentences:

1. We can understand the meaning of _____X_____ if we examine how _____X_____ differs from _____Y_____ .
2. To understand what I mean by _____X_____ it is necessary to distinguish between _____X_____ and _____Y_____ .
3. Although _____X_____ and _____Y_____ are close in meaning, they are not the same.

Content vocabulary you may wish to use:

force	freedom	residential
necessity	obligation	commercial
joy	rights	industrial
master	respect	modify
mastery	corporal punishment	modification
control	ridicule	change
own	laughter	inexorable
ownership	intention, intentional	evolve
value	psychology	starve
refuse, refusal	psychological	nourish
reject	politics	nourishment
power	political	subsist
sustenance	welfare	subsistence
liberal	starvation	
individual	commodity	

117. Definition by Negation and Contrast

One method of defining a complex concept is to explain what the concept is not. In this method the writer sets up a series of CONTRASTS. This is DEFINITION by NEGATION and DEFINITION by CONTRAST.

Use negation and contrast to explain what you mean by the following:

> persuasion
> neutrality
> homesickness
> monopoly
> pollution
> necessity

118. Ambiguity and Definition

Sometimes ambiguity can be avoided by DEFINING terms. Consider the following situation:

Mr. Y and Mrs. Y were divorced in 1960. A condition of the divorce settlement was that Mrs. Y should receive as financial settlement the revenue from her husband's investments in certain real estate as long as she did not remarry. On her remarriage this revenue would go to Mr. Y's mother. Within five years of their divorce Mrs. Y remarried her former husband. Who should get the revenue?

A. Write a brief explanation of how a clear definition of terms would have avoided this confusion.

B. To which woman would you give the money if you were the judge? Explain why.

119. Definition and Classification

In writing definition we must often make CLASSIFICATIONS of the concept we are discussing. Use CLASSIFICATION *plus any other methods* you wish to give your personal definition of:

> violence
> noise
> disrespect
> religion
> duty

120. Definition, Classification, and Explanation (Biology)

Listen to the following data.

The following are three definitions.

Predation: The most direct food relationship occurs when one organism eats another. The consumer that kills another living organism is a *predator.* The organism it kills is called the *prey.*

Scavenging: Some consumers eat dead organisms that they have not killed. This kind of consumer is called a scavenger. Sometimes animals which are normally predators act as scavengers.

Parasitism: Organisms that live on or in other living organisms and obtain their food from them are called *parasites.* The organisms that parasites live on are called *hosts.*

A. Write a short composition of CLASSIFICATION using these data. Use as your first sentence:

Organisms can be divided into three classes.

Give at least one example of each class to make sure your reader understands the contrasts among the three.

B. A predator is a factor in determining population density. Explain.

C. Explain what is meant by the statement:

"There is no such thing as an independent organism."

Use the data given above *plus* any other information which you consider relevant.

Content vocabulary you may want to use:

carnivore	interdependence
carnivorous	relationship
herbivore	extinct
herbivorous	extinction
omnivore	dense
omnivorous	density
link	prevalence
dependence	prevalent
dependent	distribution

121. Extended Definition

In an EXTENDED DEFINITION the writer includes a full explanation of the term he is discussing; he includes examples and illustrations; he discusses all the major classifications of the term he is defining.

A. Write an EXTENDED DEFINITION of *news media.*

B. Write an EXTENDED DEFINITION of *public health.*

Content vocabulary you may want to use:

publish	audience	exterminate
broadcast	censor	cure
transmit	censorship	detect
report	coverage	sickness
reporter	public opinion	illness
distribution	contagious	disease
marketing	infectious	cleanliness
sales	infect	virus
editor	"catch" a disease	bacteria
editorial	prevent	microbe
editorial policy	preventive, preventative	immunize
headline	wipe out	immunization

122. Definition: Review Exercises

A. Write a composition of DEFINITION for each of the following. Before you write, decide on which *method* or *methods* of defining you are going to use. RECALL the CONTENT of earlier exercises which you may be able to use. In addition to the data from earlier exercises, you will probably want to add material drawn from your own experience and reading.

Each of the concepts in the list has been introduced in an earlier exercise. Find the exercise(s). RECALL the VOCABULARY before you write.

CONCEPTS TO DEFINE:

extravagance	optimism
mobility	applied science
self-sufficiency	communication
superstition	chain reaction

B. Write a brief DEFINITION for each of the following. You may use any of the methods of defining that you have practiced:

> definition by example or anecdote
> definition by negation
> definition by explanation of process
> definition by contrast
> definition by classification

Each of the concepts in the list has been introduced in an earlier exercise. Find the exercise. RECALL the content, RECALL the vocabulary before you write.

CONCEPTS TO DEFINE:

immunization	school board
treaty	famine
legislature	aesthetics
colony	irrigation
taxation	ceramics
territorial expansion	precipitation

123. Writing Sentences: Review

Write a sentence for each of the following topics. Each of the topics was introduced in an earlier exercise. Your sentence must conform to the kind of logical relationship designated.

TOPIC	*RELATIONSHIP*
1. nutrition	Classification
2. transportation	Contrast
3. U.S. immigration	Cause and Effect
4. labor	Chronological Order
5. education	Definition

124. Comparison and Contrast: Review

A. Use one of the following sentences as the opening sentence of a composition of COMPARISON and CONTRAST.

Although _____ and _____ are superficially similar with respect to _____ , they are fundamentally different.

Although _____ and _____ are superficially dissimilar with respect to _____ , they are fundamentally alike.

CHOOSE from the following *TOPICS:*

two methods of travel
two kinds of news media
two kinds of entertainment
two methods of education
two kinds of public services

B. Use one of the following sentences as the opening sentence of a composition of COMPARISON.

The developments of _____ and of _____ have much in common.

or

The development of _____ is parallel to that of _____ .

CHOOSE from the following *TOPICS:*

communication
education
technology
government
economics

Introducing Hypothesis

Another major method of logical organization which every student writer must master is HYPOTHESIS. HYPOTHESIS is closely related to PREDICTION and CAUSE and EFFECT relationships. It is a special kind of INFERENCE in which we write about assumptions. In a HYPOTHESIS we assume that certain things are true in order to postulate about possibilities, or in order to investigate possibilities. The assumption of HYPOTHESES is a common factor in scientific experimentation, but it is also found in all disciplines. In writing we can talk about what is contrary to fact, both in the present and the future. We can also write about what is contrary to fact in the past. For example, we can write about what would happen if we were to have two heads right now; or what would happen if we were to have two heads tomorrow; or what would have happened if we had had two heads last week. All of these are contrary to fact, entirely speculative. HYPOTHESIS can be fun, but it can also be a matter of serious speculation.

For the non-native speaker perhaps the most difficult aspect of writing HYPOTHE-SIS is the verb tenses used in sentences using *if* and *unless*.

A. Indicate the time referred to in the following sentences of hypothesis.

    1. If we had a vacation, I would go to the beach.
    2. If Hitler had been a better general, he might have won World War II.
    3. I'd be rich if I had a million dollars.
    4. If we had been intelligent, we would have invested our money in computers.
    5. I could predict the outcome if you would only give me all the data.
    6. They wouldn't have got into trouble if they had taken their mother's advice.

B. Formulate a rule about verb tenses for the PRESENT and FUTURE in *hypothesis*.

C. Formulate a rule about verb tenses for the PAST in *hypothesis*.

Composition Exercises

125. Hypothesis (Economics/Education)

Write a composition of hypothesis for each of the following.

A. Tell what you would have done last year if you had been given a million dollars.

B. Tell what you would have changed if you could have changed your elementary school education.

Content vocabulary you may want to use:

invest	luxury	program	induction
investment	luxurious	methodology	inductive
business	spend	administration	deduction
capital	save	fundamental	deductive
charity	interest	rudiments	explore
charitable	educator	comprehensive	exploratory
philanthropy	elementary	general	exploration
philanthropic	secondary	specialize	develop
philanthropist	subject	specialized	development
millionaire	curriculum	by rote	

126. Hypothesis, Cause and Effect

> Read silently while your teacher reads aloud.

There are many problems which people would like to have solved. We often need expert knowledge in specialized fields in order to work out solutions for these problems.

A. Write five statements of HYPOTHESIS according to the following pattern.

profession   action

If I were _____ , I would _____ .

in order to find _____ .
     to solve _____ .
     to find a solution to _____ .
     to prove that _____ .
     to formulate a theory about _____ .

B. We can sometimes solve problems by experimentation. Write five statements of HYPOTHESIS according to the following patterns.

If I could experiment with _____ , I think I might be able

to prove that _____ .
to find out _____ .
to formulate a theory about _____ .

If I could devise an experiment in which _____ , I think I could show that _____ .

C. Write a paragraph in which you describe in detail what you would do to solve a certain problem. Your paragraph must show the CAUSE and EFFECT relationships of your actions.

127. Hypothesis (Autobiography)

Write a composition of HYPOTHESIS for each of the following.

A. Tell what you would do if you wanted to be considered famous in your own lifetime.

B. Tell what you would do if you wanted to be considered notorious after your death.

C. Tell what you would do if you found out that you had only one more month to live.

Content vocabulary you may want to use:

destiny	notorious	carry out	the dead
destined to	notoriety	fulfill	dead (adjective)
fate	accomplishment	succeed	death
fated to	accomplish	success	fail
fame	ambition	acclaim	failure
famous	ambitious	die	

128. Hypothesis (Science Fiction)

A. Assume the following hypothetical situation is true:

It is the year 2000 A.D. The planet earth has been invaded by a super-race from outer space. This super-race is superior to human beings technologically and has the power to destroy earth. Your task is to persuade the leaders of the super-race not to destroy the earth.

180

Write a composition in which you explain to the invaders why earth should not be destroyed.

B. If you invented a pill which could make people non-violent, what would you do with it?

Write a composition in which you discuss the actions you would take, including any constraints you would place on the uses of the pill.

Content vocabulary you may want to use:

protect	attack	intelligence
protection	destroy	master
culture	destruction	slave
customs	welfare	race, races
earth	guard	peaceful
technology	weapons	territory
beauty	system	settle
architecture	solar system	beg
literature	balance	plead
sculpture	in balance	demand
painting	friendly	translate
at peace	allies	discuss
at war	supply of _____	argue
security	biology	make an effort
resources	biological cycle	make a decision
density of population	intelligent	reach a decision

129. Hypothesis, Cause and Effect (Geography/Economics)

Examine the map and consider the following data about a hypothetical country, X Land, which is situated in a subtropical region.

area: 600 miles long, 400 miles wide
population: 4,000,000
1 large city: 750,000 population, capital
1 seaport: 500,000 population
rural population: scattered throughout plateau and foothills; some fishing villages along the coast.
terrain: (1)   coastal region with sandy beaches, dense forest, extends 50 miles inland.
             (2)   upland plateaus, 200 miles wide, good agricultural soil; 2000 ft. above sea level.
             (3)   foothills of mountains with forests, mineral deposits, rise gradually from 2000 ft. above sea level.
             (4)   mountain range 10,000-12,000 ft. above sea level.

one major river: 1/4 mile wide, navigable up to fall-line.
manufacturing: fish canning, food processing in the two cities.
natural resources: forests, fish, agriculture, silver mining, oil.
education: illiteracy rate 20%
             one university in the capital city
             compulsory education through age 10
average life span: 52 years
yearly average per capita income: $900 (U.S. dollars)

One year ago oil was discovered (see map). The government has built a road from
the seaport to the oil field. This is the first major highway in the country. Prior to
this time the river was the main transportation means and other roads were minor.

Write a composition in which you discuss the changes you think the oil discovery
and subsequent highway will bring about in the country. Consider in your composition some of the following:

         population distribution   tourism
         standard of living   manufacturing
         exports, imports   development of cities
         social customs

Ask yourself QUESTIONS before you write.

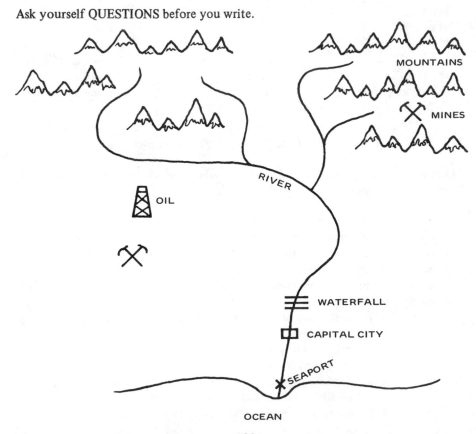

130. Comparison and Contrast (Biology)

A. Write a paragraph on the similarities and differences of PLANTS and ANIMALS.

Before you write, make a brief outline of the characteristics you will consider. For example, you should consider the following aspects:

ability to move	methods of breathing
food — what kinds, how eaten	reproduction
what cells are made of	defense
variety	life span
senses	intelligence

B. Now that you have tried to contrast animal life and plant life, you are aware of some of the difficulties involved in grouping all living things under two headings (plant and animal).

(a) Write a brief paragraph in which you summarize the problems involved in such a classification.

(b) Write three sentences of HYPOTHESIS to illustrate the difficulties involved in such a classification.

(c) Write a general descriptive statement about plants which is only seemingly true. Prove your statement is false by citing an example which REFUTES it.

Introducing Proposals

Read silently while your teacher reads aloud.

Many situations call for the writing of proposals. A written proposal is usually a plan which is offered for acceptance or rejection. It usually includes a general statement of the plan and an explanation of how the plan is to be implemented. It may include the reasons for implementing the plan, and the results expected. Written proposals may include different kinds of logical organization, such as classification, cause and effect, and prediction. When you write a proposal, choose appropriate kinds of organization.

Structure Vocabulary

I propose that

I would propose that

I propose to

It seems feasible to

It would be feasible to

It would be profitable to
expedient
imperative
disastrous
beneficial

I would suggest that
urge
demand

I would advocate that
plead for
pledge to

I would plan to

I would forbid

I would exclude

I would bar

I would prevent

I would prohibit

Composition Exercises

131. Writing Sentences of Proposal

Write sentences of proposal on each of the following topics. Try to RECALL CONTENT VOCABULARY for each topic.

1. education
2. transportation
3. government
4. pollution
5. mail delivery

Use these sentence patterns for your sentences.

                   data   name of official
                   ↓   or organization

1. Because of _____ I would propose to _____ that he

                 recommendation
                   ↓

should _____ .

                                       name of official
                   data   or organization

2. Because it is true that _____ , I would recommend that _____

                 recommendation
                   ↓

should _____ .

132. Proposal (International Problems)

Write a short composition in which you explain what you would do if you were appointed temporary head of the United Nations for one year. Assume that you are one of a very small number of candidates who might be chosen. Make your proposals as persuasive as possible.

Content vocabulary you may want to use:

take action	national	cooperation
implement	international	peace
temporary	unite	peaceful
permanent	unity	remedy

urgent	divide	equal
urgency	division	equality
necessary	human welfare	social
necessity	discrimination	authority
emergency	prejudice	organization
crisis	freedom to	appoint
crucial	freedom from	appointment
essential	society	position
solve	solution	administrator
world situation	cooperate	administration

133. Hypothesis (Pollution)

Review in your mind the information you were given in an earlier exercise about the water cycle. Look up the data and vocabulary if necessary.

A. Write a composition of HYPOTHESIS and CAUSE and EFFECT in which you discuss what would happen if the major rivers of the world became irreversibly polluted.

B. Many cities in the U.S. use salt in winter to make the roads less slippery. The salt is absorbed into the ground water system. Discuss what may happen if most of the large cities in an area continue to use salt in winter.

134. Comparison and Contrast (Economics)

A. Explain the difference between paper money and personal checks. Consider intrinsic value, general acceptability, and usefulness as a medium of exchange.

B. Explain the relative advantages and disadvantages of the barter system and the use of metal money. Keep in mind that you are restricted to one kind of money; you may not discuss paper money.

135. Classification and Explanation (Mathematics)

Use the following data to write a composition in which you CLASSIFY several number systems. First you must group the information into logical order according to class (category, kind, type). Then you must sort out the information for each group according to the *kind* of information it is.

1. The twelve-scale number system is called duo-decimal.
2. The need for numbers probably grew out of people's desire to make records of their possessions.
3. The Roman system is one of the best known of the many number systems people have invented.

4. We divide the foot into twelve inches.
5. It is easy to count numbers up to ten using our fingers.
6. The duo-decimal system is used for linear measurement.
7. The Roman system used symbols to designate groups of different sizes.
8. If a symbol of lesser value is written after one of larger value, its value is added on: VI means six, and conversely IX means nine.
9. We divide the clock into twelve hours.
10. Some American Indians kept a record of their sheep by placing in a bag a stone for each sheep.
11. V means five; X means ten; C means one hundred.
12. The Arabic system is easier to use than the Roman system.
13. The Roman system is a decimal system.
14. The Hindu-Arabic system was introduced into Europe by the Arabs about 900 A.D.
15. The day is measured in 24 hours.
16. Pictures of groups of objects can be found painted on cave walls.
17. The value of a symbol in the Arabic system depends on its position in the series.
18. The circle has 360 degrees.
19. Twelve can be divided without a remainder by more numbers than ten can.
20. Early methods of keeping records did not involve a true counting or number system; the basis of recording was matching markers with the objects to be "counted."
21. We call a number system based on tens a decimal system.
22. The duo-decimal system has some advantages over the decimal system.
23. The binary system is used by computer scientists.
24. People cut notches in sticks or made scratches on stones.
25. Later, people learned to use words to designate numbers.
26. With the Hindu-Arabic number system, any number can be written by choosing from the ten symbols in the number series 1, 2, 3, 4, 5, 6, 7, 8, 9, 0.
27. The number two is the basis of the binary system.

136. Classification (Transportation)

In writing a theme of classification about transportation, we can choose from many methods of classifying data. Transportation methods can be classified by

speed	availability
economy (cost)	beauty
type of power used	usefulness
size	etc.

Write a composition of classification about transportation. State EXPLICITLY your method of classification at the beginning of your composition. For each of your classes ENUMERATE specific examples. Use one of the following suggested opening sentences.

Modern transportation can be divided into _____ classes according to
_____ .

or

If we examine the _____ of modern vehicles, we find _____ distinct
kinds.

or

Modern transportation falls into _____ categories with respect to _____ .

Content vocabulary you may want to use:

historical	by sea	engineering
history	by land	propulsion
mechanics	terrestrial	passenger
mechanical	manual	vehicle
nuclear	by hand	vehicular
electric	velocity	traffic
electricity	practical	route
electrical	practicality	capacity
aquatic	engine	

137. Explanation (Ambiguity)

Examine the following signs.

A. Assume you must obey the instructions given by the two signs. Write five
   questions you would ask the authorities who put up the signs.

B. Write a brief paragraph in which you explain why the signs are confusing.

C. Design two new signs which you consider more satisfactory.

138. Cause and Effect Relationships: Review of Cycles/Chains

A. We have seen that cause and effect relationships are sometimes *chain reactions.*

  1. Make brief outlines of two cause and effect chain reactions. Indicate the steps for each.

  2. Choose *one* of the two chain reactions you have outlined. Write a brief paragraph of explanation of the chain reaction.

B. We have seen that cause and effect relationships are sometimes *cycles.*

  1. Make brief outlines of two cycles. Indicate the steps for each.

  2. Choose *one* of the two cycles you have outlined. Write a brief paragraph of explanation of the cycle.

C. *Post hoc* versus true cause and effect.

  1. Give three examples of a series which is only *apparently* a cause and effect relationship but which is really a *post hoc* relationship.

  2. Explain the true relationship involved in each of the series you gave as examples in 1. above.

139. Analogy and Hypothesis (Biology/Geography)

Use the following scientific theories as analogies in a short composition of HYPOTHESIS about life in outer space. Many people believe that there are living creatures on planets other than earth. If there are, can we expect them to be similar to human beings? (Keep in mind that although analogies rarely have a perfect one-to-one correspondence with the main topic, they should correspond as closely as possible. If the analogy contains a glaring inconsistency with the original topic, the writer should explain why the inconsistency is not important in any case, or should be overlooked by the reader.)

Listen to the following data.

Different animal species are native to different parts of the modern world. Scientists believe, for example, that the animal life of Australia differs so radically from that of the Orient because of geographic isolation. With isolation comes in-breeding and new species are created which cannot cross the geographic barrier. Geological studies show that Asia and Australia have been separated for seventy million years. Fossil evidence shows that at one time marsupials dominated the entire earth but their method of raising young in a pouch was not as efficient as that of modern mammals which give birth to more advanced youth. Therefore the marsupials survived in Australia, which was cut off from the other land masses before modern mammals reached it.

Introducing Personal Opinion

> Read silently while your teacher reads aloud.

Writing personal opinion is not really a new logical method of organizing written material. When we write personal opinion, we utilize all the other methods of organization. However, there is one major difference. In writing personal opinion we utilize both facts and opinions. It is essential to clearly indicate for the reader which statements are FACTS and which are OPINIONS.

As with GENERALIZATION and SPECIFICS we must be sure to support our opinions. When we write personal opinion, we CHOOSE our method(s) of organization.

Structure Vocabulary

I think
It seems to me
In my opinion
To me
I consider
I conclude that
I agree with
I disagree with
I base my opinion on
I contend that
I claim that
According to my point of view

From my point of view
In my view
I am positive (certain, sure) that
It is clear to me that
I argue that
I suppose
I assume
I don't know if
I don't know whether
If I am not mistaken
I hesitate to say

Composition Exercises

140. Personal Opinion (Education)

Write a brief composition on each of the following.

A. What do you think is the most important subject that should be taught to children in elementary school? Why?

B. Should girls have the same education as boys? Why or why not?

C. Should high school students be allowed to choose which subjects they are to study, or should they follow a prescribed curriculum? Explain your opinion.

D. Many women feel that the government should provide day-care centers for young children so that the mothers may work. What kind of day-care centers should the government provide? What kinds of children should go to day-care centers (age, health, family background, economic background, etc.)? Should the government encourage or discourage the establishment of such centers? Give your personal opinions.

141. Personal Opinion (Food)

Essentially we eat in order to provide our bodies with fuel, but for most people eating is more than a way of providing themselves with nourishment. What does eating mean to you?

142. Prediction and Personal Opinion

A. The kind of society in which human beings live has changed throughout history. What kind of a society do you think people of the future will live in? What will human beings be like in 3000 A.D.? What will their family life, their dwellings, their education, and their society be like? Write a composition in which you predict the changes that will take place between now and 3000 A.D. in human social organization.

B. What kind of a world would you like for your great-grandchildren? Describe the world you would like them to live in. Consider at least two aspects of future life: political, economic, social, psychological, educational, etc.

C. What do you think the role of the scientist will be in the year 3000 A.D.?

143. Comparison and Contrast, and Personal Opinion (News Media)

A. Write a composition in which you COMPARE and CONTRAST the relative merits of any two kinds of news media. (For example: TV and newspapers, movies and TV, magazines and newspapers).

Before you write, make a list of the criteria by which you judge news media. (For example: size of audience, depth of coverage, immediacy, etc.)

Use examples to substantiate your claims about the effectiveness of the kind of media you favor.

B. Some people protest the policies of a newspaper by canceling their subscription and writing to the editor to tell him why. Under what circumstance would you take this action? Write a composition of HYPOTHESIS and PERSONAL OPINION in which you explain what policies a newspaper or magazine would have to follow to make you take this action.

C. Write a composition of PREDICTION in which you discuss how news will be communicated in the twenty-first century.

Content vocabulary you may want to use:

editor	audience response	suppress
editorial	involvement	suppression
editorial policy	repress	control
headlines	repression	advantage
publicity	influence	advantageous
sensationalism	have influence on	directed at
advertising	rights	impact
management	express opinions	ownership
reporter	expression	responsibility
news coverage	censor	
audience	censorship	

144. Personal Opinion (Sociology)

Some scientists are experimenting with control of behavior through the implantation of electrodes in the brains of monkeys. It is possible to alter the monkeys' behavior by the application of electrical current. The animals can be made to fear what they would naturally regard favorably or to lack fear of something which previously produced fear in them. Critics say that this research poses a potential threat to human freedom and should be stopped. Write a composition in which you give your opinion of the desirability of such experiments.

Content vocabulary you may want to use:

behavior	authority	dictate	respond
behavioral	mental illness	dictator	response
experiment	psychology	authoritarian	stimulus
experimentation	psychosis	voluntary	apply
control	neurosis	involuntary	application

145. Comparison and Contrast, and Personal Opinion (Sports/Hobbies)

A. Choose two sports which you enjoy either as a spectator or as a participant. Write a composition in which you explain which you would prefer if you could be a world champion in one of the two.

B. Choose two skills you would like to learn. Write a composition in which you explain why you would prefer one rather than the other if you were allowed to choose only one.

Content vocabulary you may want to use:

movement	improvise	rough
agility	improvisation	speed
agile	conditioning	skill
interruption	contact	rules
excitement	contact sport	

146. Hypothesis and Personal Opinion (Government/Law)

A. Under what circumstances would you feel justified in killing another person? Write a composition in which you explain your viewpoint. Your composition should combine CLASSIFICATION, HYPOTHESIS, and PERSONAL OPINION.

B. What would you do if the government of the country in which a close friend lived started arresting and shooting large numbers of innocent people and refused to explain its reasons? What advice would you give your friend? What action would you take?

C. You have a friend who is a very rich man. His only child has been kidnapped. The kidnappers have contacted him and have asked for $1,000,000 in ransom money. They have warned him not to contact the police. What advice would you give your friend? What action would you take?

147. Personal Opinion (Sociology)

Write a composition of PERSONAL OPINION for each of the following.

A. You are a famous surgeon who has made a world-wide reputation for performing heart transplants. People with serious heart ailments come to your hospital from all over the world. At present there are two patients in your hospital who will die within a very few days if they do not receive a new heart. Examine the data about each patient, and decide to which one you will give the next available heart.

> Patient #1: male
> thirty-five years old
> married with six children
> sole support of his family as his wife is dead
> grocery clerk

> Patient #2: female
> eighteen years old
> unmarried
> talented violinist, genius I.Q.

Which patient should receive the heart? Why?

B. Should governments pass a law which compels people to give their bodies to hospitals on death? What safeguards would you establish for such a law?

148. Personal Opinion (Economics/Fine Arts)

A. You have been given a gift of a sum of money which you must spend in one of two ways. The money is designated either for the purchase of a painting or for the purchase of theatre tickets for twenty years. Explain which of the two you would choose, giving specific reasons for your choice. (Watch tenses!)

B. Mrs. Smith is a widow who has consulted you for advice. She has inherited $10,000 which she does not need for current expenditures. She wants to know whether she should invest the money in stocks and bonds or whether she should buy real estate as an investment. What advice would you give her? (Watch tenses!)

Content vocabulary you may want to use:

sense	structure	appreciate	return on an
senses	materials	appreciation	investment
imagine	form (noun)	scene	profit
imagination	comfort	view	property
imaginary	release	pérfect (adj.)	taxes
respond	satisfy	perféct (verb)	resale
utility	satisfaction	benefit	resale value
beauty	emotion	return (noun)	resell

194

149. Personal Opinion and Hypothesis

A. If you could spend one day with one famous person, whom would you choose? Write a composition in which you explain your choice.

B. If you could have changed one event in history, what would you have changed? Write a composition in which you tell what you would have changed and why.

C. If you could visit one country for a one-year expense paid vacation, where would you choose to go? Write a composition in which you explain your choice and what you would do during your vacation.

D. If you could have lived at one time in your country's history, which time would you have chosen to live in? Write a composition in which you tell when you would have chosen to live and why.

150. Personal Opinion, Comparison and Contrast (Geography/Sociology)

A. Where would you prefer to live: in a tropical climate or in an arctic climate? Write a composition in which you explain your preference by comparing and contrasting the desirability of the two climates.

B. Write a composition in which you explain whether you prefer to live in a large city or in a small town.

151. Comparison and Contrast, and Personal Opinion (Business)

The Amalgamated Business Machines Company, which has offices throughout the United States and in several foreign countries, has a vacancy in its administrative staff. There are two applicants for the position. Examine the summary of each applicant's credentials. Then write a report in which you tell to which candidate you would give the position and why. You must defend your choice and give reasons for your decision.

	Mrs. X	Mr. Y
Age	29	35
Marital status	married; one child (2 years old) husband is a doctor	married; 4 children (2, 4, 9, and 11 years old)
Education	B.A., M.A., in Business Admin.	B.A. in Business Admin. with minor in Economics
Health record	excellent	excellent
Church affiliation	none	Roman Catholic
Civic work	active in local Democratic party; secretary-treasurer of state Business and Professional Women's Association	Little League Baseball Coach; Member of Parent-Teacher Association
Foreign Language	fluent in Spanish and French Can read German	none
Previous experience	4 years with Central Electronics as 1) assistant personnel manager, 2) personnel manager, 3) special assistant to the president. Hasn't worked for last 3 years.	2 years as H.S. Business teacher and coach; 8 years as assistant head of accounting department in State Highway Dept; last 3 years as head of accounting office in State Highway Department.

Content vocabulary you may wish to use:

curriculum vitae	evaluation	criterion	employ
policy	object	criteria	employment
public relations	objection	prospective	employer
academic record	advantage	capability	employee
experience	disadvantage	hire	
qualification	selection	in the light of	
candidate	select	with respect to	
evaluate	appropriate	with regard to	

196

Introducing Refutation

> Read silently while your teacher reads aloud.

One particular form of PERSONAL OPINION is REFUTATION. In REFUTATION the writer proves that someone else's opinion is false. To show that the other opinion is erroneous the writer may use a variety of logical methods of organization.

Consider the following controversial opinions. Do you agree with each of them? How would you refute those you disagree with?

A. All children should be given an identical education until the age of twelve.

B. Life in a large city necessarily breeds discourtesy and alienation.

C. There is no such thing as bad luck, just bad planning and incompetence.

D. Poverty is caused by laziness.

Structure Vocabulary

true	conversely	disagree *with*
untrue		disagreement
false	infer	
falsity	inference	logic
fallacious		logically
	imply	
in error	implication	deduce
erroneous		deduction
	presume	
oppose	presumption	consistent
opposite	contradict	inconsistent
in opposition	contradiction	consistency
	contradictory	
mutually exclusive		bias
partially true	contrary	prejudice

Composition Exercises

152. Definition and Personal Opinion (Sociology)

Dictionary definitions and personal opinions do not always coincide. Consider the following dictionary definitions:

extortion: the criminal offense of using one's position or powers to obtain property, funds, or patronage to which one is not entitled.

violence: physical force exerted for the purpose of injuring, damaging, or abusing.

Using the dictionary definitions as your guide, explain if you agree or disagree with the following personal definitions. Explain clearly to each of the two people the extent to which you think his statement is or is not acceptable. Consider the kind of statement he is making: is it really a definition, is it only an example, does it require clarification or expansion, etc? In other words, put in writing what you would say to him in a discussion about his use of *extortion* and *violence*.

Mr. A: It was just extortion; that's what it was. Right before the election when we citizens could all vote on whether or not to increase the millage for the schools (that's the property tax for the upkeep of the schools, you know), the superintendent told the newspapers that if the millage didn't pass, the schools would have to go on half-days.

Mr. B: The United States is committing violence against small children. Hundreds of children go to school hungry every morning. Why doesn't the government do something about it?

You will write two compositions of ARGUMENTATION and PERSONAL OPINION.

153. Personal Opinion, Comparison and Contrast (Business)

You are offered two positions. In the first job the initial salary is high. The employer pays for health and life insurance. Every year you are granted thirty days vacation. Every month you have three sick-leave days which may be accumulated. Promotions are automatic in accordance with years of service. Salary increases are guaranteed. In the second job the salary is based strictly on accomplishment and varies from month to month according to your production. There is no maximum ceiling to the number of hours you may work. Raises and promotions are based on competition with other staff members. You may take vacations any time at your own expense. Hospital and life insurance are provided.

Write a composition in which you explain which of the two jobs you would prefer to have.

154. Classification and Personal Opinion (Sociology)

According to statistics, people who live in the U.S. are extremely mobile. Do you think mobility is a good or bad characteristic for a population to have? Consider the characteristic of mobility as it affects at least three aspects of life. Choose any three aspects you wish. Give your personal opinion of the values or disadvantages of mobility for each.

Aspects you may wish to write about:

economics	education of children
social life	politics
family life	psychology

155. Definition and Personal Opinion (Economics)

One eminent economist defines *money* as "anything that is generally acceptable as a medium of exchange." Write a composition in which you discuss to what extent you agree or disagree with this definition and why.

Content vocabulary you may want to use:

barter	valuable	seller
circulation	worth (adj.)	buyer
currency	worth (noun)	consumer
exchange	purchase (verb)	purchaser
in exchange for	purchase (noun)	intermediary
economy	check	supply
economics	credit card	demand
commodity	safe (noun)	availability
resources	safety deposit box	means (a means of_____)
transaction	deposit	medium of exchange
value	withdraw	

Introducing Discussion

Read silently while your teacher reads aloud.

The word discussion has different meanings for oral communication and written communication. In oral communication a discussion is a kind of structured, disciplined conversation. In a written discussion, on the other hand, there is only one "voice," that of the writer. When a student is asked to write a composition of discussion, he may choose any method or combination of methods of organization that he wishes. Frequently he will want to combine several methods of organization. A good student thinks not only about WHAT he is saying but also about HOW he is organizing his ideas. Use the following method to develop proficiency in writing discussion questions. Draw a margin along the right hand side of the page.

	M A R G I N

As you write, record the METHOD of organization you are using. Your teacher will check your paper for (1) CONTENT and (2) METHOD.

Try to write approximately three hundred words in thirty minutes.

Here are the instructions you are to follow in writing DISCUSSION.

BEFORE YOU WRITE:

1. RECALL CONTENT ideas and CONTENT VOCABULARY you will need. Think about earlier exercises, your own reading, your own experience.

2. Recall METHODS of organization you want to use.

3. Make ASSOCIATIONS, INFERENCES, RELATIONSHIPS. ASK YOURSELF QUESTIONS IN ENGLISH.

Composition Exercises

156. Discussion

Practice writing discussion about the following controversial topics.

A. Many people today are worried about overpopulation. Discuss the relative merits of government control of population growth and freedom of individual choice as to family size.

B. An eminent physician has said that he would not vote for a woman President of the United States because women are not fit for executive positions. Discuss.

C. Commercial television directs many of its advertisements at small children. Advertisements for candy, cereals, soft drinks, and toys are often written for an audience of children. Some critics of TV advertising consider this immoral. Discuss.

D. Discuss the relative merits of a democracy and a benevolent dictatorship in a time of national crisis.

E. Some people argue that technology has not liberated man but has enslaved him. Discuss.

Content vocabulary you may want to use:

economics	prejudicial	justify
economist	custom	justification
economic	customary	deny
education	tradition	denial of
educational	traditional	negation of
motivate	gratify	refute
motivation	gratification	refutation of
solve	acquire	natural disaster
solution	acquisition	civil disturbance
nutrition	suspend	corruption
employment	impose	corrupt (adj./verb)
implement (verb)	rights	immediacy
implementation	law	expediency
raise children	order	expedient
psychology	justice	prógress (noun)
adjustment	liberty	progreś (verb)
implication	power	paradox
susceptible	exert power	paradoxical
prejudice	exercise power	
bias	priorities	

157. Discussion (Heroes)

A. What are the essential characteristics of a national hero?

B. In every country of the world children are told stories about their national heroes. Many of these stories are told to foster patriotism. Discuss the beneficial and harmful results of this practice.

158. Discussion (Transportation)

Write a composition in which you discuss the relationship between developments in transportation (for example, planes, helicopters, hovercraft, submarines) and the nature of warfare. If you wish, you may include predictions of future effects on warfare of new transportation means.

159. Discussion (Science)

Scientists are trained to be objective while working in the laboratory. Objectivity is a desirable trait in a democracy. Therefore all students should have basic training in science. Discuss.

160. Discussion (Political Beliefs)

At one time a man had said:

> I believe students should be allowed to hear speakers of all political philos-
> ophies, even communists. Students should be allowed to make up their
> own minds.

At another time the same man said:

> I am opposed to communism because it distorts the truth.

This man was accused of being inconsistent. Was this accusation valid? Write a composition in which you discuss his consistency or inconsistency.

161. Discussion (Sociology)

Research has shown that a severely malnourished population is apathetic, unambi-tious, and lacking in energy to undertake innovations.

Historical analysis has shown that an oppressed population is most likely to revolt when they have experienced a slight improvement in their living standards.

Discuss the implications of these two facts for the planned development of an underdeveloped country. You may use specific historical examples; you may deal in hypothesis only, or you may combine the two approaches.

162. Discussion (Behavior)

The following are OPINIONS. Discuss the validity of each in a composition. You may agree, disagree, or agree only in part with the opinions listed.

A. Happiness is a matter of adjustment to one's environment.

B. People fail because they subconsciously want to fail.

C. The worst fate that can befall a person is to be bored.

163. Discussion (Education)

Write a composition of DISCUSSION about each of the following opinions. Your composition should show to what extent you agree or disagree with the statements given.

A. Young boys should be encouraged to fight.

B. Parents, not educators, should control the schools, including the establishment of curricula, rules, and management.

C. Responsibility for a child should rest solely with the child's family; the state has no right to interfere.

D. An educated person should be paid more money than an uneducated person regardless of the kind of work he does.

164. Discussion (Government/Law)

Discuss each of the following statements.

A. Violence is justified when laws are bad.

B. Smoking is bad for the health; smoke pollutes the air. Therefore smoking should be legally banned in all public places.

C. It is unfortunate that innocent civilians may be killed in wars, but since there is no way to avoid it, such deaths are justified.

D. Because human beings are naturally competitive, there will always be wars.

165. Discussion (Quotations)

Write a composition of DISCUSSION about each of the following quotations.

A. "Man is really a machine — a sensitive flexible machine whose behavior is controlled by a network in the brain."

B. "If ever a species needs to be removed for the good of the planet — we do." (Isaac Asimov)

C. "I am against 'brotherhood.' I used to make speeches about brotherhood but I never mention it anymore. Brotherhood is misleading. What we need is not brotherhood, but coexistence." (Ralph Bunche)

D. "Teachers do not change minds or personalities; they change the world in which students live."

E. "Twentieth century man is the psychological man."